COWBOYS & DOG TALES

Cowboys & Dog Tales

by
Tim O'Byrne

Caitlin Press, Inc
Box 2387
Station B
Prince George BC
V2N 2S6

Cowboys and Dog Tales
©1997 Tim O'Byrne

Caitlin Pres Inc.
Box 2387
Station B
Prince George BC   V2N 2S6

Caitlin Press acknowledges the support of the Canada Council for the Arts for our publishing program. Similarly we acknowledge the support of the Arts Council of British Columbia.

Layout and design by Vancouver Desktop Publishing
Cover design by Warren Clark Graphic Design
Index by Katherine Plett
Printed in Canada

Canadian cataloguing in publication data

O'Byrne, Tim, 1960 -
Cowboys and dog tales

Includes glossary and index.
ISBN 0-920576-65-6

1. O'Byrne, Tim, 1960– 2. Ranch life—Canada, Western 3. Cattle dogs—Canada, Western—Anecdotes. 4. Cowboys— Canada, Western—Biography. I. Title
FC3209.R3O29 1997   971.2   C97-910192-1
F1060.38.O29 1997

INTRODUCTION

EVER SINCE I WAS a kid I wanted to be out-
doors. I was interested in far away places and all
the critters that call this planet home. My face
could usually be found sandwiched between the pages of a
National Geographic while I daydreamed of walking across
the plains of Africa or paddling my way up the Amazon.

My father was a career Air Force man and was stationed
at Zwiebrucken Germany in 1960. I arrived at this point to
round out a lovely threesome of children consisting of the
eldest and meanest, Marty; our cunning and shiftless sister,
Judy; and myself. I was considered by my mother to be a
marvelous gift of pure innocence and a welcome respite
from those other two creatures.

By the time our family returned to Canada in 1963 I had
established a permanent bond with my siblings that would
be reaffirmed vigorously each time Mom wasn't looking.
Dad would be periodically stationed to a different air base
somewhere in Canada and we learned to accept the life of
growing up as Air Force Brats.

I suffered through long days of school, gazing out the
window and ignoring my teacher. In my Calgary high

school I was voted "most likely to never come back." The minute I was handed my diploma I hit the pavement and never did go back. Hell, I never even looked back. I was 17 years old and ready to go, full of all the fire that a red-headed Irishman could possess at that age.

I landed a job just west of the city at an embryo facility called Alberta Livestock Transplants or just ALT for short. These folks were busy doing complicated work on beef and dairy cattle. The crew consisted of many technicians and our gang of happy-go-lucky cattle feeders.

I started my first day in silence while one of the other guys drove me around in a canary yellow pick-up. It had more dents and craters in it than the dark side of the moon. As I sat there in my new blue jeans and crisp starched baseball cap, I had a feeling way down deep in the middle of my soul that I was about to be sucked into something, taken away from the safety and security of my family, and I would not return for a long time.

I was so very right and this is where my story begins.

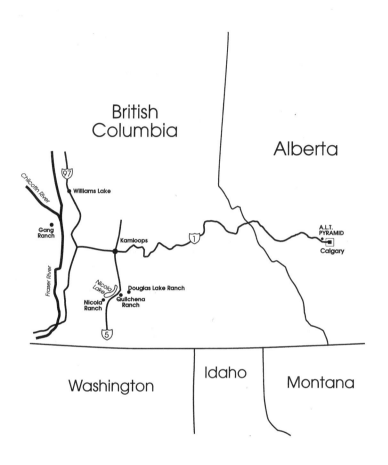

RANCHING AREAS OF WESTERN CANADA

I HAD NEVER THOUGHT MUCH about cowboys or the West. I really wanted to be a carpenter or a surgeon but both of these careers meant back to the dreaded halls of knowledge. To gain entry into agriculture it seemed as though even a criminal record was just peachy. Although not a serious lawbreaker, this suited me perfectly.

About four months after ALT put me on the payroll my job metamorphosed from feeding cattle into checking them on horseback. I was working with a young lady named Gail who was a college graduate and acting as an animal health technician at this place. She was two years my senior and what she didn't know about a cow wasn't worth knowing. While me and Gail were busy checking and sorting the cows that the veterinarians needed for their embryo work at headquarters, Stan Jacobs was doing pretty much the same thing out on the big pastures west of us. He had ten times more critters to work with than we did, but his were just commercial cows and ours were high-priced purebreds. The vet would take five or ten eggs from a purebred and then Stan would have to scramble to find ten cows from his herd that were in heat on the same day. This equation, performed daily, converted into one hell of a lot of cowboying for Stan.

One fine summer's day the powers that reign decided Stan could use some help full-time out on the pastures. The chosen one was to be me, and I nervously drove my old white pick-up into the yard of Pyramid Ranch, where he was living. Stan was a cowboy top to bottom, that was a fact. He had his own horses and his own truck and trailer. His rigging was quality and well used. He was over six feet tall and in fine shape for an old timer in his early twenties. His droopy mustache and blonde hair, combined with ice blue eyes, made him resemble a Viking warrior in a cowboy suit. A striking green and white polka dot shirt seemed to be Stan's favorite and when he topped his ensemble off with a purple silk neckrag the whole outfit just screamed, 'Look at Me.' To a full-fledged, dipped-in-shit cowboy this combination was more than acceptable but to the rest of the world it said, without apology, 'Look at me, I have no idea how to dress myself.' There were various reasons why regular people walked 'way around cowboys like Stan whenever they came to town and his clothes may have been one of them. Tucked snugly in the left breast pocket of the polka dot shirt was a round tin of Copenhagen. Wherever Stanley went, the little black tin would definitely accompany him.

I trembled as I stepped out of the truck and slammed the door with a false sense of authority. I was hoping to make an impression but Stan didn't really care about impressions too much. He just kind of stared at me like I'd left the price tag on my new brown cowboy hat. Did I leave it on? I couldn't remember and I started to panic. Beads of sweat formed on my brow and I managed to blurt out, "I'm gonna help you from now on." He was thoroughly thrilled I could tell. The right side of his mustache started to twitch and he kind of grumbled and turned on his boot heels. Up the porch steps and into the clapboard house he stomped and the screen door slammed shut with a resounding 'whack.' He left me standing there in the yard all lonely and vulnerable with nearly three hundred dollars worth of brand new cowboy gear piled high in the back of the truck.

I was about ready to bust out bawling when a couple of strange little dogs came wiggling up to me out of nowhere. "Well, Hi kids," I said, grateful for the company and began fussing with these friendly pets. The screen door squeaked open viciously. "And don't pet my dogs, dammit, I work with them!"

Whack!

The next few days and weeks were so darn much fun I could hardly stand it. One thing about being ignored—at least you're not getting yelled at all the time. Before long, Stan softened up a bit and he progressed from totally ignoring me to being mildly annoyed. He had these wonderful dogs who helped him work the cattle and they simply worshipped the ground Stan walked on. One day I thought I'd quiz him a bit.

"So what kind of a dog is that," I asked, referring to his constant companion he called "Patch."

"Australian kelpie," he replied.

"Oh, I never heard of them," I admitted. Patch was a medium brown color with a light tan mask like a raccoon and tan legs and feet. She had short hair and was not very big. Stan had a couple of other young ones hanging around also, but Patch was his most well trained and experienced. This little dog was calm, intelligent and she lived to work cows. She would look right at you with her big brown eyes like she knew just what the conversation was about. The cow dogs were all new to me and I was fascinated by them. As I asked more and more questions, Stan began to talk more freely.

He soon told me the history of the kelpie breed and how they descended from fox collies brought to Australia from Scotland in 1870. They were bred primarily as sheep dogs and were considered an excellent stock dog. Apparently some interbreeding between the early kelpie and the wild Australian dingo must have taken place, according to some breeders of the dogs. They come in an assortment of colors, mainly black, black and tan; red, red and tan; chocolate brown and smoke blue. They are muscular and built for plenty of physical activity.

God must have made cowdogs on a Wednesday when he was really rolling. They are lightweight and flawless in design, will work in almost any weather and will eat almost anything found in a normal camp. They don't talk back; they are always happy to see you and you don't have to shoe them. I came to notice this because I had lots of time to watch Stan and his dogs work. You see, Stan needed me about as much as he needed a tax assessment.

Throughout the year or so that I spent with him, I learned a great deal about cattle and horses as well as how to handle myself, more or less as a very green young cowhand. I did not see it coming at all, it must have crept right up my pant leg, but before I knew it I was bitten by the cowboy bug. Like so many other teenage boys before me, I decided that this would be my calling—the wild and free life of a cowboy. I made a vow to set out into the world, my only objective being to cover as much country and see as many things as I possibly could until I either keeled over from too much adventure or came to my senses and returned to the land of the living. In addition, I was going to redefine the word "impulsive." I succeeded.

So at the tender age of 19, I decided the best present I could give myself was 10 or 15 years of physical abuse on some of the biggest cow outfits in the West. Excessive heat and mind-numbing cold, long hard rides with little or no time off, yes, that was truly the life for me. At the end of August, I rolled my bed, threw my rigging into the truck, said adios to Stan and his tail-wagging little partners, and headed off for British Columbia's cow country.

This was the first time I had ever driven into BC. I didn't have a clue where I was going. A couple of months prior to my departure, one of the truck drivers at ALT told me to go out to the small city of Kamloops and drive 40 miles south on Highway 5. That would put me right into the big outfit country. The trip was pretty much solid Rocky Mountains until I got fifty miles outside of Kamloops. The high peaks faded gradually to low hills covered in fir and pine. The valleys and sidehills were blue with sage and the country looked dry, like desert. I drove through the city and headed south along my prescribed route.

Pretty quick the valley opened up into an expanse of gently rolling hills covered in long, golden bunchgrass. Serene blue lakes dotted the countryside. Every ten miles or so would be a beautiful ranch set quietly off the road in the shade of tall cottonwood trees. Big red barns and stately old ranch houses painted white rested proudly where they had been built almost a hundred years before.

I was so excited I almost hit the ditch. I wanted to punch cows here and I wanted to do it today. But I didn't have a clue where to start. I figured the best thing to do was just start knocking on doors. It was Sunday afternoon and you'd think somebody would be home. I took a side road that headed up to the Douglas Lake Ranch. After about 20 miles on this twisty little road I came upon the ranch clearly marked with a massive log archway over the entrance. As I had seen smaller towns in my travels I was almost overwhelmed at the size of the headquarters that I was now driving through. I got directions to the foreman's house and parked my old truck out in the driveway. I nervously walked up the steps and banged on the door.

Mike Ferguson, the cowboss, opened the door and said, "What?"

"I'm looking for work," said I. "Are you hiring?"

"Nope."

"Do you know anyone that may be hiring?"

"Try down the road 35 miles. Can't miss it, you drive right through the place."

"Thanks," I beamed.

"Yup," and he slammed the door and disappeared back inside the dark house.

"Oh goody, a lead," I thought to myself and bounced down the step with renewed vigor. Actually, I was probably feeling quite a bit better because of the fresh air. My faithful old white truck had an annoying little gas leak and prolonged time spent inside the cab with the window rolled up left me with a slightly distorted view of things. Back into the stinky truck I climbed, my intentions being to meet with destiny.

I drove down off the hill until I reached the bottom of the valley. I turned left (BC doesn't have north, south, east and west, only up, down, right or left) on the highway and proceeded onward for 15 miles until I reached the headquarters of the Nicola Ranch. Some of the buildings at the ranch were actually left over from the turn of the century townsite of Nicola. This was an incredible thing to see, not unlike a movie set. A huge Victorian mansion sat all but abandoned across from a clean tiny white church. The gray and weathered tombstones in the little cemetery beside the church leaned this way and that. Two huge barns, one red, the other white, sat on solid foundations by the creek. Surrounded by cottonwoods on a manicured lawn was a large white building marked with the words "Court House" that had obviously been converted to a residence. Many other buildings and houses, including the main cook-house, were scattered around the yard beside the highway that made an abrupt turn and headed into the town of Merritt some six miles distant.

I once again obtained directions to the cowboss's abode from an innocent bystander and proceeded post haste to his residence where I came to a halt in a cloud of dust and slammed my smelly truck into PARK. I clomped up to the front door and, with confidence, signaled my arrival.

The door opened and I introduced myself. The cowboss shook my hand and I asked if he needed a good cowboy. Apparently, I thought I was one at the time. He told me to come on in and have supper with them and we'd discuss it. His lovely wife was busy laying out a delicious looking feed of vegetables and liver. In my efforts to be polite and also to secure a job at this establishment, I boldly lied to the whole family, claiming that liver was my all-time favorite. In fact, liver did not even rate acknowledgment from my discriminating palate, but tonight I talked myself into three steaming helpings of the lovely stuff. In a performance that should have won an Oscar, I choked my way through supper, clinched the job and was rolled out in the bunkhouse later that evening, ready to start my new career as a big-outfit cowboy.

As the saying goes, there are usually three crews on a big cow outfit; one coming, one working and one going. It wasn't hard to find work since cowboys are not held in high regard as irreplaceable professionals. They come and go like stray dogs and at times there seems to be 'way too many hanging around. Then, when you need them most, you can't find any. Some will stay on an outfit a year or two at a time, others will stay a few months, then drift off, only to show up again at a later date.

By the time I got there, most of the guys who were working the country were pretty good hands. A lot of them used dogs and relied heavily on them for help in the timber. Of course, me being as green as last night's cabbage, about all I could do was shut up and watch and maybe jump in there and try to help every now and again.

I spent my first few months getting kicked or dragged or bucked off. I also tripped over lots of things and dropped numerous heavy, bone-crushing objects on my foot. This seemed to keep the crew amused and eased the tension a bit.

Meanwhile, back in Alberta, rambling fever must have hit Stan because he panicked and quit the country. Several days later, he and Patch surfaced out where I was working. The ranch needed another man and he fit the bill. We were both pretty thrilled to be punching cows together again.

The work involved on this ranch was mostly moving cattle around on horseback. We had lots of horses to ride, supplied by the company. The 2700 head of cattle the ranch owned were scattered in the bush country around the town of Merritt, BC. It was a lot for me and Stan to take in.

The cattle that called this place home spent a large part of their lives up in the hills and valleys away from the irrigated hay meadows of the main ranches. Most times it was a challenging game of hide-and-seek, with us cowboys being *it*. These old cows would hang out in only the select areas of the rough country. Most of the hills were completely covered in jack pine, 80 feet tall, with little or no grass growing under their dark canopy.

Cattle trails through the quiet bush would lead from one natural meadow to the next. These meadows may be rich in native grasses and plants and range in size from a few acres to several square miles. Some meadows were wet and boggy and grew thick mats of swamp grass. The cattle would not usually eat this tough stuff until late in the fall when there would be no more tempting green forage around.

The high mountain meadows up above the timberline were often desolate but always beautiful and very fragile. The cows would only venture this high on the nicest days of summer to escape the many mosquitoes and deer flies lurking in the damp bush. A multitude of tiny alpine flowers grew very close to the ground and one would surely miss their bashful beauty if he did not inspect them on hands and knees.

The darkest part of the bush and certainly the scariest were the silent spruce swamps. Here, in the low black soil loomed moss covered spruce trees, gnarled and menacing. Scarcely a critter, domestic or wild, ever ventured far up into a spruce swamp although almost all cattle and game trails skirted the edge of one at some point.

The mountains and hills were home to dozens of hidden

lakes, canyons and creek beds. Although the moose, deer and bears in the area knew their way around, our cows did not lead us into these remote spots too often, choosing wisely to keep to the well-traveled cow routes of previous years.

As the timbered hills faded into the open grasslands of lower altitudes, the country transformed itself into a cow's paradise of gentle grazing near plentiful lakes and creeks. Huge yellow pine trees stood here and there in isolation, and the thick tangle of red willow and rose bushes choked the draws.

The cowboys had to handle their horses and cattle in this rough country and for me, it proved quite challenging.

Soon it was time to gather the cattle and wean the calves. Fall works came and went. Me and Stan were about all used up, yet happier than two pet hamsters.

Little Patchie was living it up as well. There were so many cows and so much country she had a shit-eatin' grin on her face all fall and halfway into winter. Us cowboys mostly rode through to doctor calves and yearlings or move cowherds all winter. This particular one, 1980-81, was mild enough not to have killed any of us.

Pretty quick spring rolled around and the calves started popping. We earned our keep during this period and learned a lot as well.

One morning as the crew was working cattle at the ranch headquarters, a single cow broke from the confines of the corral system and ran out into the traffic on the highway that snaked through the valley. Patch tried valiantly to get in front of the cow, but was hit by a vehicle before she had a chance. Tragically, she was killed instantly, leaving the entire crew in complete shock. We all knew how much this little dog meant to Stan. She was another member of our crew, and we were very sorry to lose her in this way. There have been many partnerships through the years, but not many would compare with theirs.

Rarely was more than a gentle word or soft whistle ever relayed to Patch. She did her part with class and intelligence. Now she was gone. Stan took her away that afternoon and laid her to rest under a big tree that stood solemn guard on a hill top. He went alone. When her small body had been covered in dirt Stan peeled some bark off the huge tree and carved PATCH deep into the bare white wood. After a quiet moment he mounted his horse and headed slowly back down the hill towards the ranch. The rest of us finished the day's work in silence, then returned to the bunkhouse.

Goddam that highway! As I sat by myself on the couch, I sipped on a bottle of whiskey and remembered. Good old Patch. What a character. My mind drifted back to two winters ago, back in Alberta when me and Stan were holed up at Pyramid Ranch. We were feeding a bunch of cows for ALT and generally laying low. Stan had to rim out for Oklahoma for awhile, so he left me in charge of the place and his precious dogs while he was gone. He had been gone a couple of days when one night, Patch came up missing. No panic, she knew where home and the food dish was.

By suppertime the next night, still no Patch. The weather was gettin' a little frosty, and I began to worry about her. After a week of still no Patch, I began to worry about my own self when Stan found out I let his little buddy run off during such cold weather. I thought about the Witness Protection Program. Maybe they could help me find a new identity in another town somewhere. I looked high and low for that damn dog and just could not find her anywhere. After about eight days I had totally given up. Surely she was frozen to death in a ditch somewhere.

In a hopeless daze, for some reason I drove around back of the feedlot. There was a big bloated frozen dead cow back there, lying on her side with all four legs pointing straight towards the heavens. She had died the week before but the man at the rendering plant hadn't come to get her because of the weather, so we had dragged her out of the pen and into the field and just left her till things warmed up a bit.

Well, I'd been around out back 50 times that week but always on foot or horseback, never in the pick-up. As I drove past this poor dead cow, who pokes her head up out of the hind end but Patch. There she is, like a possum in the garbage can, obviously quite pleased to have the first visitors to her new winter home. She had eaten her way through the back door and liked the place so much she decided to stay. That is, until she heard the sound of the pick-up coming. I don't think she really understood why I was so glad to see her. She was so fat I could hardly load her into the back of the truck and when I got her back to the house, I never let her out of my sight until Stan returned home. Of course, she did add her own charming ambiance to the shack after she warmed up. After all, she *was* living inside a dead cow for a week.

Stan was unaware of my ordeal because I downplayed the whole thing when he got back home. Everyone was happy now, and that was the main thing.

Today it was over. All that remained were good memories. I learned then that I had to be ready for what will happen in the years ahead because if you make a commitment to have these dogs, you must be prepared to lose them. That realization did not make this day any easier.

AFTER A YEAR OR SO, I figured that I had come to know about all there was to know about punching cows, so in my infinite wisdom I decided to take on a new, bigger challenge. I was going to get me a dog.

What could be so hard about training one; after all, I already knew most of the good cuss words. Besides, I seemed to have a natural affinity with animals. I hadn't been bucked off in weeks and I could tell that my peers secretly envied my newly acquired 'unity' with horses. Maybe I was sort of destined to be an animal trainer of the highest regard. In retrospect, I did not realize back then that possessing a higher IQ than the animal you were attempting to train was an asset. No worries though, I was confident in my ignorance and was determined to become a dog man of distinction.

Stan heard through the grapevine that there was a fellow over in the city of Vernon who was raising kelpies and had some good pups for sale. So with rubber chequebooks in hand, we set off to track this gentleman down. We found him on his acreage just outside of town, busy tending

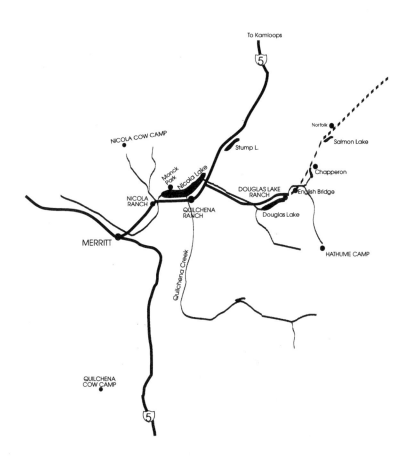

MERRITT AREA RANCHES,
BRITISH COLUMBIA

his many dogs who were staked out and tied up all over the place. There were fresh batches of pups and not-so-fresh ones, old ones and pregnant ones. They all seemed pretty happy to see us, even though we hadn't been formally introduced yet.

I was positive that I would keep my dignity amongst strangers and maybe stand there like an adult, rubbing my chin thoughtfully for a moment, then stating in low, confident tones, "Yes, I'll choose that one." But in reality, I ended up like a little kid, out of the truck before it even stopped, taking long strides over to the pups, where I was immediately mauled. I wanted to take them all home, but understood that wasn't possible. The owner of the dogs came over to greet us, and after handshakes all the way around and the usual weather talk, we went shopping. Stan, of course, knew exactly what he wanted. He stood there, thoughtfully rubbing his chin, then declared, "How about that one." He picked a little fuzzy brown female with tan mask and legs. She was cute as a bug's ear.

I didn't have a clue what I was after, so the man walked over to a nine-month-old male that was staked out and said, "Here's a gooder." That's Aussie talk, this guy was straight from Australia and had worked big cattle and sheep stations down there. So I guess he knew what a "gooder" was. This particular pup had the exact same paint job as the one Stan picked. This colour scheme seemed to be common amongst kelpies.

Grazing quietly nearby were five young bulls, all quite innocent and unsuspecting. The fellow reached down, unsnapped the chain, and in his Aussie accent yelled, "GO GET EEM, CLIFFIE!" Well, little "Cliffie" obviously hadn't been off his chain in a week or two, and he lit out of there like a torpedo about two inches off the ground. That closest bull never had a chance. Cliffie took a Hollywood leap at him from about 20 feet out, mouth wide open and hit him dead in the ribs with a vengeance. Mr. Bull came wide awake, his eyes like fried eggs and he spit his mouthful of grass clear across his other four buddies. One big beller and he reached up and cow-kicked Little Cliffie clear across the field. Little Cliffie rolled end over end into the weeds, completely happy with all the attention he was getting. The bulls, meanwhile, had rimmed out for the far corner of that little pasture. They stood there, trembling with shock, their day having been completely ruined.

Cliffie came trotting back with tail wagging and a mouthful of hair, quite proud of himself. Of course, I just had to have this little devil, so not wanting to have anything screw up the deal, I signed my real name to this particular cheque.

We loaded up, talked more weather, said goodbyes all the way around and off we went to set the world on fire.

Stanley's pup was christened "Nellie" and I changed poor Cliffie's name to "Tickerdog." I have no idea where that came from but it sounded good at the time and it was easy to shout, something I had to consider because I couldn't whistle very well. The name stuck and soon we became great old friends.

I T WAS THE END OF September and we were preparing to start our fall works. This is a busy and
exciting time of gathering cattle, making re-rides
looking for missing cows and working with the really big
herds. In my mind, it's probably the best time to be punching
cows on a big outfit because you are usually in camp with
your buddies and it's almost like a race to get all your work
done before the snow comes. Anything can happen and
usually does. Big plans are liable to change at a moment's
notice, depending on the weather and whatever the cattle
decide to do. This just makes things that much more interesting to a cowhand because most of them thrive on a
challenge.

We had a few weeks or so to get ready for the major
works, so I took this opportunity to start Tickerdog on some
basic training techniques. Due to the fact that I did not
possess one milligram of dog training ability, we both spent
some long moments just kind of staring blankly at each
other, wondering exactly what the other had in mind.

We had some yearling steers captured down at the
working pens, and they were supposed to stay there for a

week or so until we were ready to ship them. So one evening I decided to take my new partner down, stake him out in the pen and feed him there. Of course, this way he would get aggressive towards the cattle if they came close to his dog dish. Good in theory, lousy in reality with this particular dog. Man, oh, man, he took that personally; having to stay overnight in that pen with these big soggy steers. The cowdog must truly regard cattle as a species quite low on the food chain, somewhere below cats and maybe above reptiles. The minute I left the pen he began his indignant complaining and did not cease until I arrived back the next morning. I had built a makeshift shelter in the corner where he could climb up and get away from the steers if he had to. When I got out of the truck and strolled over to greet him, he wouldn't even come out of his little house and say good morning or anything. He just kind of looked away from me with the same kind of expression on his face that your wife gets when you forget her birthday. But finally I made friends with him again, and we started working with the steers.

We had a simple program. I would open the gate into the next pen and we would work on foot. I would get Tickerdog to do what he could to get the cattle moving out the gate and into the next pen. Then once we were in there, we'd reverse the procedure and put the cattle back in the original pen.

This worked real slick for several reasons. It may be better to start young dogs on dry stock. This means any type of cattle as long as it is not cows with calves. As a natural protection instinct, a cow will defend her calf against most any varmint, especially a yappy cowdog. Imagine how a thundering, bawling, vengeful 1200-pound cow can shatter a 30-pound pup's confidence. But the dry stock, especially big fat steers, can be quite eager to play as a group and they would willingly go through the gate for us at the slightest provocation. Of course this made Ticker's chest swell with pride and his face would be beaming as he trotted towards the gate after the steers. I'm sure he thought that he alone had done this remarkable feat, and he must have felt that any dog such as him that could send twenty-five thousand pounds of beef stampeding in terror should not be under-estimated.

Another reason for this method of starting a pup is the cattle are confined in close quarters with only one way out through the open gate. When they see the gate and start to go, the whole group will go. When the pup sees that what he is doing out there makes the cattle go through the gate and he is praised at the empty pen, he begins to see that what he does is for a reason. There is a result at the end of his work and he is praised. You can help him also, being on the ground yourself like that. If you were outside the confines of the pen to start with, the pup can chase all the cattle he wants, but he will not develop the ability to reason for himself if there is no direction or purpose for chasing the cattle. Tickerdog figured this out right away, and like any good kelpie, took this as his calling and dove into it passionately.

At the end of our training sessions, it was back on the chain and as I drove away, he cussed me out again to no avail. This went on for several days and nights, and I could see that he wasn't going to let up. After a week I realized that back where he came from being tied up wasn't bad because his whole family was right there beside him. But now he didn't have a pack leader. Hell, he didn't even have a pack and he certainly had no intentions of bonding to those steers. He was lonely, but not that lonely! Finally, I gave in, mostly because the whole east end of the ranch couldn't sleep at night with him barking constantly and people were threatening me with lawsuits. So in a fit of compassion, I took him back to the shack with me where he instantly came to realize that I was pack leader and he was the devoted pack—that is until later years when the title of "Leader" was constantly being wrestled back and forth between us.

Sometimes I would only be leader as long as whatever it was we were up to corresponded with his agenda. Other times he would declare himself "pack leader" for awhile and, believe me, he would march to his own band for a couple of days leaving me totally exasperated.

After I gave in and for all the years we were partnered up, I never did get that little bugger to tie up anymore. It was simply beneath him and that was that. Consequently he had free run of all the places I worked on, free choice of the garbage and any other trouble he could get into, leaving me to pay for the damages and make apologies.

By now with our crash course dog training over, fall works was well under way. I'm sure most professional dog trainers would like to choke me after reading about my "training program," but at the time I was blissfully unaware that there was any more to it than that and I set out to give Tickerdog just what every decent cowdog needs—10,000 miles behind a horse. This was definitely something I could do, because trotting horses was about all we were good at anyway. As with most performance animals, you have to take some of the wind out of their sails before their minds are in any condition to learn anything. And for eager cow-dogs, there's nothing like a 10-mile jog first thing in the morning to loosen them up and take the edge off.

I took Tickerdog with me that fall as he was big enough to go, being about a year old already. Sometimes he'd lag behind and sometimes he would have a hard time relating to me way up there on a horse. He would, as all pups do, follow the wrong horse without looking up to see who was riding it, but all in all he didn't hold me back too much. The only thing he really hated was having to swim across a cold creek, of which there are many in BC's cow country. The cattle and horses and other dogs would just plow right through and never look back leaving Tickerdog moaning and groaning on the other side. As he ran around complaining, the cowherd, cowboys and me would begin to disappear in the bush and everything would grow quiet again. Sure that he would be left behind, he would throw his paws up in the air and yell, "What the hell," and belly flop into the cold water. Up on the other side he would shake violently then take up hot pursuit of the bunch who had figured out by now not to miss him. He never did learn to like swimming creeks and avoided them all throughout his life if he could.

After a month or so of gathering cows, it was time to bring everything in to be worked. All the cattle are brought close to the working pens and are usually rodeared—or held up—in a corner somewhere. It would not be unusual on some big outfits to have a herd totalling 1200 or 1500 cows along with their calves, numerous bulls and neighbour's cows, etc. So counting calves, bulls and cows there might be 2500 animals in one rodear with maybe 10 cowboys spaced out evenly around the herd to hold them. On a cow outfit, you never count calves as part of your overall count. If you say "I work on a 3000-head cow outfit," that means there are 3000 mother cows. But there are also 2700 calves, and

there are 800 young heifers destined to become calf pro-
ducing cows next year. Finally, there might be 175 or so
bulls. So actually, in total, there may be 6700 animals in all.
But cowmen only count the mature females when referring to carrying capacity of a particular ranch, and yearling heifers and bulls are regarded as something like a
support group. Calves are always with the cows as a cow-
calf unit. That is to say 3000 cows or cow/calf units. We
just take for granted if you've got 3000 cows, you damn
well better have 2800 calves sucking them, 'cause if you
don't, you're in for one hell of a bad surprise when ship-
ping time rolls around.

The first thing the bosses usually start working out of
one of these big rodears are the bulls. Bulls don't like to be
confined or mixed up in a herd like that for too long. Pretty
soon they start to fight amongst themselves and raise hell in
the herd, running over and scattering other animals. Sometimes the foreman will ask his cowboys to keep the herd
"loose," meaning he wants the cowboys to stay back away
from the herd and give them lots of room to settle. If the
cattle are crowded, the cows will lose their calves in the herd.
It will be hard to work the neighbour's cattle out and
eventually the whole herd will become hard to hold as cows
try to break out and go in search of their calves.

The bulls, as with all the cattle, are identified by the
brand and/or the particular ear ID of the ranch. The ranch
bulls are located and the boss will poke them out of the
rodear. While the rest hold the herd, a couple or three
cowhands will head off and gather up all the bulls that the
boss has just worked and pen them somewhere. When they
arrive back at the herd, after completing this task, the boss
or maybe even a neighbour who has come to help will be

asked by the boss to go into the rodear and work out any strays. This is the reason the herd must be rodeared loosely, in order that the cows and calves can stay paired and stray cows can be worked out with their calves. These big rodears are usually run on some strict, unwritten rules. No one enters the herd unless he is instructed to by the boss, neighbours included. A cowhand who for some reason disturbs the herd or yells out his observations for all to hear will be frowned upon greatly.

Every young cowhand soon learns that if the cowboss needs your opinion or help, he'll most certainly ask for it. They also learn that these old boys never need your opinion or help and the best place to be is invisible until someone calls for you.

Once the cattle—be it pairs or yearlings, orphaned calves or bulls—that don't belong to the ranch are worked out, you are left with a "clean" herd. This means all cows, calves and yearlings belong to the outfit, with the exception of one or two the boss may have missed while working a rodear that size. No worries though, because remember that eager young cowhand that just couldn't keep his mouth shut before? Well, he'll almost surely spot any critter out of place once you start weaning and he'll darn sure let everyone know that he's seen him.

The big herd is now safe to bring into the smaller pens to wean or strip the calves. Now the fun starts. Bawling, screaming, running, cussing. The herd is all mixed up now and you can't even hear yourself think. Cowboys split up in groups of three or four and start to work the cattle in the myriad of sorting pens. Most big outfits work their cattle on horseback all the time. Some places may not, though. I always tended to get mixed up with them that did.

So now you've got several groups of cowboys doing their own jobs, either stripping calves or working out the yearlings, or sorting the fresh weaned calves into the two sex groups, steers and heifers. All this work can get a little complex to orchestrate at times, and it seems you never have enough pens, even if you've got a hundred. The cowhands communicate a lot in hand signals now because the bawling is just too loud to talk over. It's a very exciting time, the culmination of a whole year's efforts. Depending on the size of the herd and type of facilities, this work may take several days to even weeks. There are just as many different ways to do this job as there are days in the year. The result, though, is almost always the same. The neighbour's cattle are returned to their rightful owners, intact, healthy and unharmed. The ranch calves are weaned off into several different groups. Steer calves are sorted and are either sold in several different weight classes or kept to be sold the next fall as yearlings. Heifer calves are sorted two ways. The best are kept to be bred the next year and as they go into the main cow herd, an equal number of cows too old or crippled come out as culls. These culls are sold for slaughter. This completes a never-ending circle. A range cow usually will quit being productive around twelve to fifteen years of age. Every year as these culls are sold to slaughter, new ones must take their place. These big outfit cows must travel farther and work harder in a year than their small farm counterparts, thus their life expectancy dwindles.

The other half of the heifer calves will be sold as feeder cattle in their respective weight classes, and will be fed to slaughter, as will all steer calves, or they may be kept as grass cattle and sold the next fall as yearlings. Big outfits rarely if ever keep their own calves for bulls as to avoid inbreeding problems. So you can figure all male calves and half the female calves go down the road at some point in time.

After the calves are taken care of, the cows must be put through the chute. They usually go through only once a year in order to get their annual vaccinations for various bovine diseases. It is at this time that the cattle may be pregnancy tested by a veterinarian or health technician. All this cow/chute work seems timed nicely because first of all the cows are already penned and the calves weaned. All the cows were bred in June and July and the chute work takes place in November and December. This means the fetus in the cow is well into its second trimester, making it easy to detect by a veterinarian using a rectal palpation of the uterus. But the fetus isn't too far along as to be in any danger of injury from the cows being crowded and banged through the chute.

A good vet can "preg check" up to 800 cows a day if the facilities are good and the cowboys keep them coming. The boss will usually keep the pregnant ones unless they are obvious cripples, or "gummers." A gummer is a cow with few teeth left in her mouth. This is common in aged cattle. They have a hard time keeping their weight up because they can't chew their grub properly. Weight loss and poor feed conversion lead to loss of pregnancy and a cow that comes home in the fall without a kid ain't much good to anybody.

A good vet can usually figure out whether the fetus he is feeling is old enough or young enough to be born within the usual two month calving period. The boss will tell him when the bulls were turned out with the cows, as they are kept separate over the winter and spring to avoid the big cow herd calving during all seasons. The breeding and calving of a big cow herd must be closely synchronized if you are to attain the end result of a crop of even-aged and even-sized calves. It is very hard to sell a pen of mismatched big and small calves. You lose money that way, but the buyers will pay the going rate for calves that are close together in weight and conformation. If all the cows are not exposed to bulls until, let's say, June 1, they will usually be bred within six weeks and when next spring rolls around, they will usually calve within six weeks. Hence, your calf crop will be all roughly the same age and you can expect to brand 80% of your calf crop in six weeks. And so the circle goes, only a little more complex than my explanation of it. Of course this means your bull herd must be kept down at headquarters until June.

Imagine this, a couple of hundred bulls with nothing else on their minds but green grass and a little action. Many a farm foreman, while trying to keep a herd of unruly bulls out of the hay meadows, has gone over the edge to that special place where there are really big butterflies and flowers and it's summer all the time.

Usually around the end of May, the ranch manager will send the farm foreman and his wife off to town and the nearest bar where hard liquor will be consumed in copious quantities, mournful stories of renegade, disrespectful bulls stomping irrigation equipment to smithereens will be told and retold, and all frustrations will be vented. Then about the first of June, the cowboys will come down from their camps in the early hours of the morning and try to quietly move the bulls to their summer range.

The cows that are open (not pregnant) or that the vet has declared bred too late to produce an old enough calf are usually shipped for slaughter. The boss may re-evaluate some within this class, and if they are good young cows, he may give them another chance next year to get bred properly. Sometimes some of the three-year-old cows won't get bred, so they will be kept again another year because they are too young to get rid of. But in their fourth year, they are expected to be back on line and produce a calf every year.

It was during this cow work in the chutes that I used Tickerdog for his real first ranch work. I would bring fifteen or so cows out of the pen with his help and we would put them up into the small "A" shaped pen that led to the chute. These cows now that their calves were sorted and gone were less formidable and had nothing to protect, so it turned out to be excellent stock to work my pup on. And, of course, fifteen cows through the gate and into the pen, back for another fifteen and so on was excellent repetition for Ticker.

We did this three days running, and throughout those days, Ticker was threatened, stomped, kicked and mowed down by cows, all the while just blooming from all the lovely treatment he was receiving. At the end of fall works, he was battered, bruised, bloody, muddy, and looked like hell. But through all the mud caked on him he was smiling like he'd just paid cash for a new Cadillac. He loved this stuff and he was gonna do it forever, and by God, nobody better get in his way.

T HE BIG CATTLE RANCHES of the West have one thing in common—rough country and lots of it. The cattle are turned out into areas that have the grass and water to support them. When you are talking about a 3000-head cow outfit, the cattle are not run in one big herd fanning out in all directions and roaming at will. In fact, they are run as many separate herds. Some particular breeds of cows, such as the Black Angus, may make up 25% of the cow population. The ranch breeding program may call for them to be bred to a specific breed of bull in order to obtain the desired breed and type of calf. After this particular herd is built, it then spends most of the spring, summer and fall in its designated range area, and is allowed to be bred without any undesired bulls entering its country. Yearling steers are sometimes turned out in an area of the ranch which may be steeper or a bit rougher because they spread out more and will climb around to utilize the grass better than a cow with a calf. A cow is basically a lazy animal who will do only what is necessary to stay alive and is quite content to park her big fat butt one hundred yards from the nearest water hole and camp out with her buddies for the summer. That is why most cattle watering areas look like a parking lot. It is built into a cow to do this and there is nothing anyone can do about it.

The yearling replacement heifers will usually be bred for the first time to special, handpicked bulls. The bulls may be chosen on conformation, breed or maybe what weight the bull was at birth. The whole program is designed to give the heifer a small calf to deliver. This is her first time calving and most ranchers will do anything to avoid problems, which usually mean losses in terms of cattle and money. Also, it is not fair to the heifer to breed her to something she can't handle. So the bulls must do their part genetically and not produce monster-sized calves.

Some ranchers use past records to help choose their bulls for this job. If the bull has records dating back to his birth date, and the birth weight is indicated as light, not heavy, there is a good chance this bull will throw light birth weight calves as well, which is the desired effect.

All these heifers are sent to summer with their bulls into their own designated area. These different areas may be separated by fences, but more often on the big outfits, the natural barriers of the country will be what stops the drifting around. There may be a valley with meadows running up country with a river on one side that cattle won't even think about trying, and mountains at the top running all the way down the other side that most critters would leave alone. She's not into much sightseeing or mountain climbing, save for a few adventurous types—usually those pesky neighbour's cows who always seem to show up when you need them least. Actually, your average cow has the IQ of a ripe watermelon.

A water bucket only holds so much water. If you try to put too much in, it just spills out all over the place and makes a big mess. And so it is with a cow's brain. Almost 95% of it is filled with instincts and there is precious little room left over for creative thought. If too much knowledge were accidentally packed in there, who knows what havoc would be wreaked upon the ranch. So, she just spends her days doing what cows do best, eating, drinking and lying there chewing her cud with her eyes closed.

In the spring, when the sun starts to warm things up a bit and the green grass starts to grow, the cow begins to think about that nice quiet little meadow a way back up in the timber where she and ten of her closest girlfriends take the kids to spend the summer. Ah, the life. And one day soon she's gonna go back up there and not you nor the Williams Lake Stampede are gonna stop her. And so, these cows will spend their summer and fall in their little paradise with only a rare glimpse of a cowboy and the occasional visit from the neighbourhood romeo.

Then, one night in October, it will snow just a tiny bit, $1/15$ of an inch. You can almost look out over the hills and see the little brain lights come on. Sure enough, that wonderful cow and 750 of her best pals will show up three days later, pressed against the fence of the nearest hay meadow. Some cows will have hiked 25 miles straight, stopping only long enough to take a piss, with the bewildered but ever faithful calves marching right along behind them. Once an instinct is called up on the screen from deep within the hollows of the cow's mind, they take on all of the attributes of an Olympian performing one of the seven tasks. So with heads down and tails swinging, 80% of the cow herd arrives home in the fall, right on time and quite proud of themselves. Oh, incidentally, they would like to see you on that full feed wagon any time within the next 10 minutes.

Now, the other 20% are still out there. These are the free thinkers. Some are stupid, some stubborn and some are big old bulls who just want to be left alone forever. This latter bunch is about $1/5$ of my reason for living. I would eat Brussel sprouts for a week if someone promised me I could go on a bull hunt with my cowboy buddies. Some bulls, especially if they've beat the odd gunsel in the bush a couple of times, can be very difficult to get under control. Once the rancher finds out where they are hiding, usually by spotting them out of a plane or chopper, the cowhands will drive out and trailer their horses and dogs as close as they can get. Once out and mounted, they fly off in a barking, steaming mob and try to pick up the bulls' tracks. This always takes place in the dead of winter because the bulls are usually the last ones out of the bush. Once a hot track is locked onto anything goes. The bull will take the cowboys and dogs on a grand tour of the country, making sure to spend at least some time in an area where the tree branches are weighed down with snow. The bull goes under but the cowboys explode through these trees, and gallons of snow always go down the back of their necks and form a glacier in that area of the butt that they can't get to right now because there's no time. Bulls like this will do anything to beat the cowboys. They will run off into the steepest country or hit for the thickest willow brush and hole up. They'll go through fences, corrals, gates, crossroads, anything. I've met one or two I'm sure would have tried to get a flight out of there if they thought they could fit through that little metal detector gate at the airport. Of course, all this action is just grand for us cowboys and dogs, and soon enough the dogs have got him. Then, one rope, two, then three are on him and the game is over. It takes a lot of ropes to slow one of these big buggers down. Some bulls weigh as much as 2600 pounds. Give him an attitude and they command a little respect. A general rule of thumb we use when working with one of these badass bulls is when you rope him, it doesn't matter what you got, a front foot, an ear lobe, nuts, it don't matter, just dally. You won't see a lot of pretty roping at these kinds of rodeos. They usually take place in bush so thick that the dogs have to back out to bark. Besides, everybody's hands are so froze by now, they are lucky to be able to even make a loop. Nonetheless, Mr. Bull is captured and one way or another is loaded up and taken home. This kind of treatment usually cures his bad habits and next time he sees a cowboy and a dog he probably won't try to beat them.

Luckily only two percent of bulls are this hard to get home. Most of the ones that are left out in the early winter are just holed up under some big old tree somewhere. All you gotta do is find them, ride up and introduce yourself. Basically you have to turn this one's light on manually, as it is not automatic like the rest. He will look up at you and say, "Is it that time already?"

"Give or take a couple of months, you bonehead," you grumble. "Besides, I couldn't think of a better way to spend New Year's Day than to come dig your frozen butt out of the snow." And off you go, with your grateful, polite bull leading the way through the trail in the snow you so graciously laid out for him.

You generally won't find many cows out this late. If you do, they will usually be in a little group and quite easy to get. They tend to hang in areas they will survive in, like frozen swamp meadows or river breaks. Sometimes you'll jump a little bunch, perhaps five cows and five calves. Four pair will belong to the ranch and one pair might be from the neighbours, who live in the opposite direction. They are all pretty glad to see you, and anytime this late if you find cattle, you take them home to get them on feed whether they are yours or not. Any man who works out a neighbour's cow in November several miles from nowhere and leaves her, then heads for home with his cows is sort of like the guy who gets out early Saturday morning with his new 700 hp snowblower and blows six metric tons of snow onto his neighbour's driveway. There ought to be laws against these things, and the riff-raff who are found guilty of these crimes should do hard time.

So now you've found these cows and you head straight east towards the ranch and warmth, feed, and hot drinks for the cowboy. This all sounds fine to the cows, for about 500 yards anyway, when "bink," there goes that light again, except it's going on in the neighbour's cow this time. "This is all so wonderful," she seems to say, "but if we're gonna go home, let's go home. Home is that-a-way."

Now we have four eastbound cows, one westbound cow and one thoroughly pissed cowhand in the middle. How the heck can a cow be wrong and be right at the same time? It sure takes a lot of time and effort to explain to the bitch that if she just trusts you, it will all work out. So, several hours and several hundred attempts to bend her, you've finally got her convinced it's all for the better and off you go. The four ranch cows are relieved that all the hold-up is over and they can get on with business. The neighbour's cow has submitted grudgingly to stay with the bunch. The cowboy feels somewhat better mentally, having vented much of the pent up anger and frustration of the last week at this stray beast who has caused him so much grief.

If you get the gist of all this and all the work that a cowhand has to do to keep the outfit together, it may be easy to appreciate how a good dog or dogs can make it easier on the crew. In the same respect, one can also see how a not-so-good dog can affect the overall performance in a negative way.

With all this country to cover and all the places the cattle hide out in, the dogs play a big role in finding and handling wayward cattle. Most big outfit cowherds have been worked by dogs all their lives, and in a sense get trained to being handled this way. It's like having a shotgun under the bar. You don't have to haul it out very often. Everybody knows it's there and acts accordingly. So it is with the cows. A herd that has seen and felt the wrath of a pack of angry cowdogs will rarely challenge them. The dogs, if worked properly, act as a deterrent and the work goes smoothly and quietly.

There are several different breeds of dogs compatible with working cattle. Each one has its own peculiarities common to the breed. Through the miracles of mother nature when these or other breeds mingle in the biblical sense, anything can happen. Some of the best dogs you could ask for are products of a sordid fling. Of course, some pups inherit the worst qualities from both sides of the family. These pups enjoy careers of limited time spans in the beef cattle industry.

The border collie is an excellent breed for working cattle as well as sheep. Any that I've seen, and they are by far the most popular up here, were smart, level headed and extremely faithful. They seem to be quiet dogs and are very quick. They work well close to their master and are always watching him for the next command. However, some of them seem to be very sensitive and don't take verbal criticism well. All in all, they are excellent and you could probably cross them with a raccoon and the pups would work cows.

There are red collies and black collies. Of course, they are not solid colours, but red and white or black and white. Some have one or two blue eyes. There are three attributes cowdogs possess along with natural cow-working ability—bite, the ability and willingness to bite cattle at the proper times; bark, the ability to bark at cattle at the proper times; and eye, the ability to stare face to face with an animal until the animal literally backs down and turns in defeat. Border collies possess all three of these.

Blue heelers were uncommon on the big outfits I chose to work on. The two or three that I had the pleasure to meet were very lovable little characters. They were as tough as the Australian outback from where they came. The blue heeler is neither scared nor intimidated by a mere cow and is more than willing to take one or two of the huge beasts on to the death if need be. They are good little dogs to have around camp because we could collect their teeth that had been kicked out and were lying all over to use them for bingo markers.

A couple of guys I worked with had huntaways or huntaway crosses. The huntaway is from New Zealand. It's a big dog with a big, deep powerful bark. This bark just scares the living daylights out of cattle and when the dogs let loose, cows will climb trees to get out of there. The huntaway crosses I've seen were extremely smart dogs and worked unbelievably well.

The catahoula is an excellent tracking and head dog. A head dog is one who naturally goes to the head or front of cattle and stops or turns them. This is extremely useful in thick bush where cattle will rim out and a cowboy can't get around them. The heel dog won't help much in this instance and will probably drive the cattle farther into the bush. But a good head dog can easily outrun the cattle and go around them, barking to get them to stop or turn. The catahoula will do this as well as track cattle if you put them on a hot track. You don't see many up north here, but they are quite common in the southern half of the United States.

The kelpies of course, are being used but are not all that common. They too, possess eye, bite and bark or any combination thereof. They can get a little thick in the head sometimes, but as a rule are best left to work the herd independently but with a little supervision. No one breed is better than the rest, in my opinion. Much more depends on the personality and talent of the individual dog and the manner in which he has been trained. Most will agree that a good cowdog must have natural cow-working instinct, at least one of the bite/bark/eye attributes. Very important on the list is physical stamina. The dog must have the conformation in his legs to be able to stand up to all those miles. The pads on the feet must be durable and not be susceptible to cracks and wear. The dog must be able to take the heat and cold in extremes. One in thirty dogs will quit working on a hot day, usually just when you need them most. I've seen some that needed to be packed back to camp while their counterparts easily made it through the day. These types of dogs are a liability and are extremely rare. Survival of the fittest certainly applies here.

A good, fit, healthy dog will be able to handle the long

circles on the big outfits until around ten years of age. You rarely see dogs any older than that still putting in the kinds of days that it takes to keep up to the cowboys. Usually in the fall there will be lots of pen work and short circles to keep the old-timers happy. I've seen a few old grizzled up, half crippled "retirees" lead the pack out for a short circle through the hay meadows in the late fall. Through the glint in their eyes and the wiggle in their walk, you can tell that in their own minds, this is just a little bit like heaven. They parade around proudly in front of any pups that may be present, dripping with authority. Not much different than the human situation, I'd say, and besides, these old dogs certainly have earned the right to act with such dignity. I feel it is a strong testimony to how important work is to these cowdogs and why they absolutely can't function without it.

T HE EARLY 1980S WERE times of unlimited freedom for me and my cowboy compadres. If one were to look at the letters we wrote to one another and retrace the return addresses and postmarks, it would clearly show that neither commitment nor international boundaries meant much to us in those days.

Around May of '82 I drifted down into northern Nevada and picked up work on the TS, one of the big desert outfits around Battle Mountain. The ranches in this country still pulled branding wagons out in the spring. Of course, an actual horse drawn wagon would be a rare thing indeed, most of them having been replaced with small portable cook trailers which could be pulled with a pick-up truck.

In this country, the wagon cook as well as the buckaroos would sleep in their own individual canvas tents or teepee tents. The average day between spring and fall would start early so that we could avoid the heat of the afternoon. Cattle will not work well in the heat and cowboys have always taken advantage of early breakfasts to make the work easier for them. Consequently, we saddle our horses in the dark most days.

I took Ticker along with me on this trip to the States and he didn't seem to care what country he was in as long as he had a cow in front of him.

After a month or so of punching cows at headquarters, they moved me out to the wagon crew, who by now were well under way branding out in the desert.

This was definitely wide open country. Huge flat ancient lake beds covered in waist-high sagebrush were surrounded by dry barren mountains. The grass in this country existed mainly under the cover of the sagebrush plants and the few areas seeded to a mixture of tame grass. Up in the mountain areas, gentle side hills of native grasses, sage and juniper trees grew in the heat. It seemed like the sun was always shining in this desert country. The water was scarce in places, but there was enough of it in the form of creeks, dugouts and wind- or diesel-operated pump stations.

Flash flood water had carved deep arroyos in the desert floor and concealed under sage brush, these gulleys ran sometimes for miles. Some were six feet deep and only 10 feet across, making it difficult to find a suitable crossing.

Scorpions, deer mice and porcupines shared this lovely chunk of Nevada with us, and it is here that we made our camp.

Our wagon cook was a genial chap that went by the name of "One Fingered Bob." He only weighed about 90 pounds and had kind of an Asian look to him. One Fingered Bob was about half bald and was missing one of his index fingers. Damn, old Bob was a happy little man and although he probably made a lot of miles on a barstool he sure was a good cook. He was always making pies or braided donuts for us in that rickety old wagon of his. Bob had an ancient transistor radio that was playing at all times on a high shelf in his cook wagon. The speaker must have blown in the late '60s and the static and hissing that spewed forth from that old piece of junk was enough to make a man quit cowboying and go back to college. Now this was back in the days when Princess Diana was fixing to marry Prince Charming and whenever anything came over Bob's old radio about this big event, he made us hush up so he could hear every single detail.

Old One Fingered Bob took a liking to Tickerdog right away. Soon, though I began to notice some serious problems with my pooch. During the first few hours of each day, Ticker would have to stop every so often and puke his guts out. After a week or so of this, I was getting a bit concerned till one morning, just as we were saddling up in the dark as usual, I saw our gracious cook feeding my dog copious quantities of greasy breakfast leftovers. To a human, this is about the same as having Thanksgiving Dinner over at Aunt Vivian's and then running the Boston Marathon. Most wagon cooks are polite and will spring at the opportunity to help their fellow man. They are smug in their knowledge that the number one rule of cowboying is "Don't Piss The Cook Off." They would eagerly help the young cowhand adjust to his new life away from his mother by cooking all his favorite meals at a moment's notice, as long as it was frijoles. So when kindly asked, good old Bob refrained from feeding my poor dog half to death and directed his energies elsewhere.

About a month or so later, the big Fourth of July festivities were about to commence all over the country. We wound down our works so we could head into town with a clear conscience and raise a little hell for a few days. Four of us decided to book a motel room in Elko and share it, and since not one of us had any intention of ever using it to sleep in, there was no worry of overcrowding. Since the whole ranch had become an instant ghost town on Friday afternoon, I couldn't very well leave Ticker there. Who knows where he would bugger off to? I decided to take him along with us. He could live in the air-conditioned motel room by day and camp out overnight in the truck. Everyone else was too busy gearing up to party to care anyway, so in a flurry of wild-rags and high-topped boots, off we went. No place in the world compares to Elko when you've been on the wagon for three weeks, and as soon as we checked in and paid for our precious room in cash for four luxurious days, we set off in several different directions to get into trouble, vowing to meet at the Commercial Hotel at least sometime within the next 24 hours. And meet we did, in the early morning hours of the next day. After trading stories and a round of drinks, we set off to our beloved motel room for showers, TV and a little rest and then back at 'er. One of the guys had quit the party early the night before and went back to the room where he lay in a coma while we drank our breakfast.

We first realized something was wrong when we walked up to our room door and were met by a very angry Mexican cleaning lady. I found out that you don't necessarily have to know a language to understand what's being said, and the way she threatened us with that bucket of soapy water made me not want to stick my head through the door. But I did anyway and lo and behold, there on the bed, oblivious to all this craziness, lay our missing companion, *Playboy* magazine draped across his chest, beer cans strewn all over and a bag of taco chips by his side. Beside the bed was an empty carton of guacamole dip. We had no idea what guacamole dip could do to a dog's constitution, and the three of us stood awestruck in the doorway and gazed slowly around at the walls, the floor, and the ceiling, much the way tourists would view Michelangelo's Sistine Chapel. And there, sitting terrified in the corner was poor Tickerdog with a painful look on his face and about 10 pounds lighter. That dip must have shot through him like hot oil through a garden hose. It was everywhere, I mean, everywhere. All eyes slowly rotated back to me. When the motel manager arrived at the crime scene and promptly evicted us, without any hope of recovering our deposit for the next three days, things went from bad to worse. We found out that this once beautiful room was in fact the last room available for the holiday weekend in all of Elko, and that's when they decided to kill me. Already an expert at talking my way out of jackpots that Ticker had put me in, I hustled the boys off and bought them several well-needed rounds of drinks at the nearest establishment and tried to persuade them to postpone my cold-blooded murder for awhile. After much deliberation, they decided that the sheer magnitude of paperwork involved in a homicide investigation of a Canadian in Elko would spoil their weekend, so with backslaps all around, we raised our glasses and toasted our good fortune. After all, now that we didn't have a room to go back to, there was no reason to leave all this partying. I felt very fortunate to have survived that episode. It was a close one, but don't forget, that was back in 1982. We had never won the World Series yet and Americans still thought Canadians were pretty cool.

WENDELL STOLZFUS WAS just a gangly kid fresh out of high school when he left rural Alberta and headed west, colliding head-on with me and Stan in the Nicola Ranch cookhouse. We didn't care much for the name "Wendell," so we renamed him "Puck" because of his great love for the gentle sport of hockey.

Me and Stan heard through the ranch grapevine that poor Puck was here for two months on a trial basis only. After his probation period was over, he would either be put on the payroll in ink, or the foreman would give his skinny little ass the boot.

Of course, once Stan and I got wind of this, a sinister plot began to incubate. With careful calculations only master mathematicians like us could pull off, we estimated to the precise day when Puck's trial run was to be over. We made our circles rather quickly that day and made certain to beat Puck back to camp. Knowing full well our foreman would be nowhere to be found till the next day, we hastily threw Puck's meagre belongings into his moth-eaten warbag and rolled his sorry-looking bedroll. Then we dragged the whole mess out of the bunkhouse and piled it for all to see in the middle of the camp. We then put our feet up on the bunkhouse porch and waited.

Sure enough, the rest of the crew rode in as we expected they would, with an unsuspecting Puck right in the middle of them. He left the pack and rode over towards his pathetic little pile of gear, looked at it, then at us.

"What's all this?" he asked in a strained, high pitched voice.

Stan put down his magazine and spat his toothpick out.

"It's all over for you kid, the boss came up this afternoon and said you was no good. He wants you outta here by supper time."

I could hardly keep my giggles in, so I pulled my copy of *Western Horseman* up high to shield my face. We fully expected the guy to bust out bawling and whimpering like a little kid. It was supposed to be really funny. But we sort of underestimated Puck's gutsy attitude.

"Well, the hell with you, all of you!" he blared. With that he jerked the riggin' off his horse and kicked him loose. Then he started dragging his gear towards his pick-up, muttering four letter words under his breath all the while.

Me and Stan just kinda looked goofy at one another. We both knew that the only way this story was gonna have a happy ending was if one of us went down there and explained our little joke to the guy. It wouldn't look good if he was mad at us the rest of the year, and besides, we kind of liked having him around. After all, if he wasn't here, who would ride all the useless horses in the cavvy?

So I was duly appointed to go down and iron this affair out and go I did. Soon all was settled and me and Stan more or less accepted this independent young renegade into our esteemed ranks.

Puck's family originated in the States, so he had the privilege of crossing the border as he wished. He used this to his advantage, working on some of the biggest outfits in Oregon, Nevada and Arizona in his youth. Of course, he wouldn't be half the hand he is today without me and Stan having guided his every move from our Head Office.

After his family moved to Alberta from Pennsylvania, he grew up on his dad's dairy farm surrounded by a passle of sisters and a few brothers. He did a little rodeo stint in his teens and damn sure wasn't scared to ride any horse that was handed to him. He always worked through the day with a cheery smile plastered to his face, ready and willing to tackle anything as long as he could do it his way, which was usually pretty good anyhow.

In late September of '82 while I was working in Nevada, Puck and Stan decided to drive down and look me up. Our crew had just finished branding a bunch of calves that afternoon and we were very thirsty. Like a mirage across the desert came a dark blue Chevy van, dust billowing out behind it. Us cowhands stared off across the heat waves trying to figure out who the hell it was, coming way out here. Pretty quick the van came to a dusty stop right in front of us. The doors opened and out popped Stan and Puck, just beaming like proud parents of a nine-pound baby boy.

"We brought you a present," declared Stan.

"It was tough to get it across the border, but we told the guard you were gonna be needing this right about now so he let us through," added Puck.

They opened the side door to the van and stood back. A

barely audible gasp was heard as there, through the dust and heat, me and my buckaroo buddies laid eyes on the most beautiful thing we had ever seen. Two full cases of wonderful Canadian beer packed snugly into a cooler of sparkling white ice. A cheer arose from the crowd as we dug in whole-heartedly. Puck and Stan knew they'd made themselves a half dozen instant permanent friends.

As we cooled ourselves on crisp Canadian brew, we swapped lies and gossip. They stayed and rode with us for a week just for fun and when it was time for them to leave, they convinced me to come back up to BC with them. Fall works were just about to start and there was a good chance we could all get hired on the same outfit up there. At the same time, the wagon boss was pulling at them from the other end to try and get them to roll their beds out here and finish up the year. But in the end, we all decided to pull the pin. After another frivolous good-bye to Elko (this time I visited under an assumed name), it was handshakes all around and we left Nevada in a cloud of dust.

The three of us ended up in the back country camp of Bob Munsey. He ran the Voght Valley Division of Nicola Ranch so I was back amongst familiar people and surroundings. Bob was going to change our attitudes a bit about this line of work. Bob was from down in the desert country of southeast Oregon. He was a powerful man in his 50s when we crossed paths with a casual outlook on life that began to rub off on us young pups. He talked with a definite southwest drawl, complete with all the phrasing and jargon that went with it. His cheerful wife Pat was from the western States as well, and she acted somewhat like den mother to us as she kept us fed that fall during the works. Her house was always very tidy and well decorated in western fashion, and she held a career as a school teacher in town.

Bob was heavy set with dark rimmed glasses and large, tough hands. He always managed to keep his sense of humour while teaching the tricks of the trade. We learned how to laugh at our own foolish mistakes and not be set back by them. Rank horses seemed to be Bob's specialty and he acted as though he'd been raised in a barn full of them. He'd always get a big grin on if any of our shitters tried to buck us off, and sometimes he'd take the worst ones and put some miles on them just for the fun of it.

Bob was also a very independent sort and apparently it came to him at an early age. When he was about four years old, his family lived in a house on the outskirts of a dry, dusty Oregon town. One hot day, shortly before lunch time, little Bob ran into some domestic trouble. The outcome of the dispute didn't sit well with him, so he rolled up his paltry possessions into a handkerchief, tied it on a stick and slung it over his shoulder. One last stop in the front room to say goodbye to his mean old family and then out the door and down the road he went, headed towards town and the promise of a better life. Well, the family just kind of looked at one another and then went on with their business of fixing lunch, not giving little Bob so much as a second thought.

They had sat down to their meal and were about half way through it when poor Bob come a-skulking through the front door and into the dining room. Nobody said a word or even cast him a casual glance as he stood forlornly beside his place at the table, which was set the same as if he had never left. Finally, in a desperate bid to make the whole family see that the long lost runaway had come back at last, he said as only a four year old can say and remain serious, "Well, I see you still got the same old dog."

Yes, it was truly a cruel world out there. But us cowboys were put here to make it a better place.

For all of Bob's attributes, he had one glaring character flaw. He believed that no man should pay more than five dollars for a cowdog. He always seemed to have two or three following him around in those days, and about all the talking he ever did during the day was to say, "Jiggs, Brutus, come buh-hind" every three minutes. Jiggs and Brutus were Bob's black and white collie partners, Jiggs being the fatter, fluffy young one. Both dogs were perpetually happy with their lot in life, which I secretly thought to be amusing.

To complete Bob's crew was his venerable old potlicker Blue, who in his prime, would have been the canine equivalent of a mountain gorilla. Even though he was crippled in the hips and his trot was reduced to a painful wiggle, his jaws and powerful chest sent a shiver up my spine whenever I looked at him. He must have been a big bad bully on the block in his youth. Those dogs never did listen to a word Bob said and were just happy to be living on the same planet as him. Every now and again they'd get to run a badass bull out of some willows or whatever. Then the "logging" would start and them dogs would bring that bull on the run with bush and small trees flying everywhere.

After weaning that fall, we were loading the last of the calves up the chute and onto a truck. I was standing outside the chute with a bar, ready to put it behind the last calf and lock them in as they went up. Ticker was down there trying to work and I was so nervous he'd do something wrong that all week I'd been constantly calling him off. As the last of the calves were being brought up the chute, I called Ticker off again as the trucker pushed them up. Just then, Bob calls out to me, "For Christ's sake, kid, let the son of a bitch work. That's what you paid $5000 for, isn't it?"

I turned my head for one second, totally dumbfounded that he had actually addressed me personally. When I looked back to what I was doing, there lying in a heap at the bottom of the chute was the truck driver. As I looked away I accidentally poked him in the ribs with that heavy steel bar. His mouth was open and he was trying to say some very bad things to me, but he didn't have any wind. The severity of his injuries assured me of a hasty getaway. He probably would have been too sore to beat me anyway. I'm sure the boys would be able to calm him down just fine, so I went someplace a little quieter to ponder the day's events.

Tim on Deuce at Douglas Lake's Dry Farm Camp with Puck, Forty and his brother Flintstone. This is what cowboys do if they ever get a day off.

Little curious kelpie pups from one of Stan's females at Nicola Ranch.

Tim on the TS, Battle Mountain, Nevada.

The TS Wagon camped at Horse Creek, Alberta.

Tim and Chris at Chapperon, Douglas Lake, British Columbia.

Ticker at Douglas Lake, British Columbia.

THE SPRING OF 1983 found me and TD (Tickerdog) on the payroll of the spectacular Quilchena
Cattle Company. This ranch was owned by the
Rose family and was famous for its gorgeous historic Quilchena Hotel on the shores of Nicola Lake about 15 miles
north of Merritt, British Columbia.

TD was getting pretty used to his daily diet of long miles
and cows. He had begun to mellow somewhat and was
beginning to mature into a level-headed reliable dog at
work as well as a gentle friend during off hours. Living
closely with these dogs as we did, all the peculiar habits and
personality traits began to come to light, such as Ticker's
trademark technique of drinking water. Three slurps and
a pause. Three slurps and a pause. I knew it was him in the
middle of the night in a bunkhouse full of cowboys and dogs
by his unique style of lapping it up.

I had begun to notice also that this dog refused to play,
period. While other dogs would play ball or frisbee with
their partners, Ticker would just stare at any object tossed
his way and choose to ignore it along with the idiot who

threw it at him. This was a free country and I did not press the issue with him.

I was sent to calve cows out in an area of open country that bordered some rough timber. I would haul my horse up in the truck, unload and ride through the cows during the day. I prowled around through these cows for about five weeks or so, till they were about done calving. We left them for a couple of weeks while we were starting to brand some of the early calves. Finally, I got back into that piece of country one day only to find a bear had killed and ate a few calves. I had left one carcass and just rode up over a little swale and who do I bump into but Mr. Bear himself. It was early afternoon and getting kind of warm out. This big old bear was used to getting his way and wasn't in any hurry to rim out. I wasn't too sure how my shitter was going to react to this because I hadn't been riding him more than a few weeks. Soon enough, the chase was on, though. This old bear had been dogged before as we were about to find out. Down into the bottom of the deepest trashiest draw he loped with TD hot on his tail. It was too thick for my tastes but I could follow the edge of the draw as it snaked its way up into the bush. After much crashing and barking, finally I spot the pursuer and pursuee.

This was early in the spring now, and old Mr. Bear wasn't in any condition to be doing cross country jogging here. Pretty soon it got to be a little too much for him and he just quit and plopped down on his fat butt. Well, this is all just fine by Tickerdog, and he collapsed in a panting heap 15 feet behind. I was monitoring all the action closely from above and soon enough the bear picked himself up, straightened his tie and off he went. Same with Tickerdog and more barking and crashing. Pretty soon all's quiet. There they were again, two out-of-shape idiots sitting there, gasping for air. This went on for about twenty minutes until we worked our way up and out of the easy country and Mr. Bear waltzed into the thick stuff, never to be seen again. That old bugger never even considered treeing and that's probably why he lived as long as he did. And Ticker never really did make a great effort to catch this bear, which is probably why he lived as long as he did.

As spring wore on, the branding crews were starting to form up. There were lots of men in camp now, and with them, were lots of dogs.

Branding time on big outfits can take up the best part of six weeks or so and towards the end can become rather tedious on the crew. Usually small herds are built from the area in which the cows are calved in. The herd will be moved across country to turnout pastures and corralled. Branding and vaccination of calves takes place and after all is settled, the crew rides back to camp and begins the process the next day. After 10 days of this, your average cowboy's mind turns to mush during the long, hot, boring ride home. All jokes and stories have been told twice already, and everyone pretty much is mired deep in their own thoughts.

It was about the sixth time we had taken 125 pairs up the long valley trail from the O'Rourke holding field to the Courtney Lake branding trap. After the days work, eight or nine of us cowboys were riding back down the valley towards Quilchena's Triangle Ranch. As usual, our six or seven dogs were out front when suddenly they all took off in one barking, foaming mass. Down the draw about a half a mile was a bear up to his belly button in a berry patch. He had red berry juice smeared all around his lips and a look on his face like he'd just farted in church. Things were looking pretty grim because the nearest tree was a lone bull pine about 1000 yards away. He lit out of there like a dragster and pretty quick it turned into a full blown, cold-jawed downhill runaway; with the bear in the lead, a pack of seething cowdogs closing in, and a small herd of freshly awakened cowboys and horses bringing up the rear. We had to hurry up and get to our dogs before they got to the bear. Lord knows we didn't want anyone to get hurt, least of all our poor bear who up until now was just minding his own business.

Whoever said bears can't run downhill has obviously never seen a bear with a reason to run downhill. Believe me, this bear had a damn good reason.

Huffing and puffing, he made it to the safety of the big bull pine and was 20 feet up and hugging it when the dogs piled up in a tangle at the bottom. What a mess. Still running on high octane, the dogs turned their frustration on losing the bear onto one another. This was quickly turning into the biggest damn dogfight I'd ever witnessed. By the time we showed up, they were just boiling at the base of that big old tree. A couple of the guys bailed off their horses, grabbed big sticks and waded in there. These dogfights can get a little expensive because good dogs can get crippled up if they are left to fight it out, due to the fact that the main gang will pick on one until he's all beat up, and then turn on another one, and so on. They had to be stopped.

As the boys fumbled around, swatting any dogs that came within batting range, the bear had regained his composure a bit and stretched out on a limb far above the melee. As he looked on with a mixture of curiosity and boredom, we finally got the pack broke up and back to their respective corners. We mounted up and tipped our hats to the bear, leaving him to come down on his own time. The party was over and the whole miserable bunch of us resumed our journey back to camp.

Later that summer, I took a job as the sole cowboy on a small grazing permit used by Quilchena Cattle Co. and Pike Mountain Ranch. It was a pretty cushy job. All I had to do was keep the 350 or so cows pushed up into the back country, keep the salt out and the fences up. I chose to start early and beat the heat each day.

One afternoon as I was trotting my horse back to camp, Tickerdog was out in front on the trail as usual. All at once a little black bear came smoking down off the hill and across the trail and down into the jackpines. He caught us both by surprise. TD just took off hell bent for election around this bear and bent him back towards me. As Ticker chased him as fast as they both could run, the bear suddenly swung around and opened up his arms. TD had nowhere to go but straight in and that little bear just hugged the living daylights out of him. Down the bank and through the pine needles they rolled in a ball of black fuzz. They smacked up against a tree and when this broke the bear's grip. Ticker came shooting out of there like his tail was on fire. He ran back to me, then turned around and we both watched our little bear haul ass down the draw and out of sight. There was always a surprise waiting for you each and every day it seemed. We looked at each other and shrugged, continuing on our way home.

Later that summer I decided a town trip was needed since I had about 11 months of dirty laundry to do. It was shortly after noon on Saturday when I finished my short circle. I had ridden down one of the hay meadow fence lines to check things out. Back at camp I turned my shitter loose and fed all the horses up real good since I wouldn't be back until late Sunday evening. I took a quick whore's bath and dumped a coffee can full of dog chow into Ticker's dish.

"See ya, Buddy," I said as I patted his dirty head and scratched his back. He probably couldn't wait for me to get the hell outta there and he could have the place to himself for the weekend.

When I hit Merritt later that afternoon, I went directly to the laundromat. Once I was inside I filled half a dozen machines with assorted work duds that looked and smelled as if they had been excavated from an Egyptian tomb.

The Coldwater Hotel was just across the street so since my clothes didn't need me anymore I bounced over there for a beer. This was a meeting place of sorts for all us young cowboys on Saturday afternoon and soon I was knee deep in a bullshit session. It was several hours later when I staggered back to the laundromat to put my rags in the dryers. I let them tumble a couple of times and pulled them outta there. I had learned that if you dry your clothes for too long the buttons and zippers fly off. I pushed the damp clothes back into my big warbag and took the whole mess back out to the truck. I really needed a woman, maybe even a wife to do all this stuff because I couldn't help notice it was really cutting into my beer drinking time. Back to the bar I loped to finish off the night with the rest of the boys and when it came to an end I stumbled out to the parking lot and unrolled my bed in the back of the truck.

Sunday morning arrived viciously and without warning. The sun's evil rays had me at their mercy as I lay trapped in the hot steel truck bed. Why wouldn't the Coldwater Hotel people come out and give me water to drink? The same people that smiled broadly as they sold me beer after beer last night were nowhere to be found. My head hurt. My glasses were completely lost amid the clutter of beer cans and bedding and I needed them in order to find them.

When I had finally pulled myself together and cleaned up at the corner Esso station I figured I had better put in an appearance at the local church. My family had been Irish Catholics since St. John the Baptist was a little kid. Although I descended from a long line of fierce Celtic warriors of the Clan O'Byrne we had a secret that few people knew about. The clan was actually ruled from within by the wise, forth-right and rock steady women. And by Christ when the elder O'Byrne women said it was time to go to church, there was no argument. Mass was cleverly scheduled for the morning immediately after Saturday night to allow us cowboys a chance to redeem ourselves carrying fresh memories of the night before. We could then relax and enjoy a conscience-free week. After church, I picked up a newspaper and pointed my rusty truck back up the mountain towards camp. As I pulled up in front of the little trailer, Ticker was lying on the porch. I got out of the truck and slammed the door. Some rusty pieces fell off the side but that didn't worry me because they were bio-degradable. I strolled over to my little partner and said, "Geez, Tickie, you look like I feel." I nudged him with the toe of my boot.

He felt and moved like something a taxidermist would use to hold the front door open on a hot day. I knelt down for a closer examination and was horrified to learn that poor Ticker's pupils were completely dilated, he was nearly in a coma and about $3/5$ths rigor-mortised. Quickly I opened the passenger door to my truck, being careful not to knock any more rust pieces off lest they be structurally important.

I fired TD inside like a postal worker loading a box

marked 'Fragile.' Gingerly I closed the door, scurried around to my side, got in and burned out of the ranch yard, pedalling my tired old truck as fast as I could in the direction of the Merritt Vet Clinic some 40 miles back down the mountain.

My mind was racing as I kept an eye on the road and the other on my comatose hound. He just lay there, suspended in animation with drool leaking out his open mouth and onto the custom imitation vinyl seat of my classic vehicle. Odd, I had a cousin that looked just like that. He worked for the government.

Did Tickerdog tangle with a rabid critter that showed up at camp one night? Dogs sometimes look like this when they've got a puppy stuck inside but I expertly ruled that out. Had aliens arrived over the weekend and extracted Tickerdog's central nervous system?

Long before I could figure any of this out I arrived at the vet clinic. Shit, I forgot it was Sunday and the place was deserted. I drove over to the motel down the street and gave the vet a call. Almost before I hung up the phone, good old Dr. Purdy was unlocking the door of the clinic back up the street, possibly confirming a rumour I had heard that he lived in a cave out behind the building. I rocketed back over there and with the utmost care I lifted Ticker's limp body off the truck and packed him up the stairs and into the clinic. Neurotic pet owners weren't allowed into the back so I paced nervously in front of the cat wormer rack. Cats! "What the hell good were cats?" I thought as I stopped and looked at a picture of a happy cat on a box of wormer. No wonder the son of a bitch is happy, he probably just woke up from his nap. Frantically I continued my pacing.

After what seemed like hours, Dr. Purdy appeared with a small bottle of pills.

"Acute garbage poisoning," he declared and headed straight for the cash register.

"A-what?" my voice said.

"He got into the garbage somewhere. Sometimes when a dog gets into the garbage he will gorge on things that may not be good for him and all the toxins end up in the liver and the dog blows a breaker."

I was stunned. Time stood still. The silence was shattered abruptly as the cash register sprang to life with its evil beeping.

"Let's see, Sunday call, overnight observation." His voice started out monotone at the beginning of each category and then jumped a couple of notes higher for the last word or two, like humans do when they are tallying up a real huge bill.

"Over night obser-VATION, one bottle of little LIVER PILLS." The cash register taunted me with its incessant beeps, laughing beeps now, getting louder and louder.

"Thank you, come again." Dr. Purdy smiled as I left.

That frickin' dog! I didn't even know if I was gonna come back tomorrow and claim his sorry ass. "Let Dr. Purdy keep him for a couple of months and see how much money it takes to keep him going," I grumbled to myself.

A week later Tickerdog was back at camp and 100% fixed. I had to hold a gun to his head to get him to swallow one of those little pills but I finally figured out that if I hid it in a piece of cheese it would be devoured within hundredths of a second. For me this was the beginning of a long and expensive dance with veterinarians all over the BC interior. For Ticker it was just another beautiful day in Cowboy Land.

THE BEGINNING OF 1984 found me and Ticker back down in the Nicola Valley. I hired on for my second spring at Quilchena and was enjoying both the surroundings and the boys I had to work with. This ranch also had the best horses around and that spring we trotted some long miles in nice open country. One of the hazards of working out in the grasslands of the BC interior in springtime was dealing with ticks. The Rocky Mountain spotted woodtick is common in this area. These eight legged little critters live on the grass and bushes and just sort of hang out and do whatever it is ticks do until some animal wanders by and they can catch a ride. When they are finally aboard, they make a meal of their gracious host for a week or so. In the process, some ticks will secrete a toxin back into the animal which paralyses them. It only takes a few ticks to knock down a 1000-pound cow. So us cowboys were instructed to always watch carefully as we rode around for any cattle which may be lying down paralysed. If we found one, all we had to do was find the little culprits and pick them off the animal. Very soon, the cow will rise shakily to its feet and in most cases will recover within hours.

Of course, since us, our horses and our dogs were out where the action was, we too could get a tick on us and suffer the same fate. The danger was there, though unlikely, and in typical cowboy fashion, some of us worked this to our advantage by making sure our girlfriends checked us out top to bottom before tucking us in at night. The old-timers told us to hang our clothes on the back of a chair overnight. In the morning, the ticks will have crawled to the top and will be sitting there waiting for you. We always seemed to have just as much luck leaving our clothes scattered in a trail on the floor of the bunkhouse. No worries anyway, because I could not imagine any form of life lasting too long in any of my clothes at the time.

One particular beautiful spring morning, we were up and halfway out the door. I called for Tickerdog to come with us and as I watched him try to get up, I saw that something was wrong. I told the boys to go ahead without me and I went back to my paralysed mutt lying there on the floor. When he'd try to get up he would capsize and just lay there with a dreamy look on his face like he was in love or something. The first thing that crossed my mind was the garbage.

Even though there were three of us in the bunkhouse that spring, and we were cooking for ourselves, the stuff we made wasn't fit for a dog to eat when it was fresh, let alone after two days in the garbage. But the rest of us were OK, so I ruled that out. I started looking for ticks.

When a tick is in his normal state, he is sort of a flat disk-shaped affair with legs and a mouth. When he attaches himself, he blows up to 10 times his size with the host's blood. They are easy to find when they are like that, but I didn't find any on Ticker, so I phoned our local vet. After howdies, he thanked me for providing funding to make construction of the new addition to his clinic possible, and I told him no problem, that's what I was out here working for. He wasn't surprised, but actually sounded a bit pleased in a sinister sort of way when I told him that Wonderdog was in serious trouble again. In my mind I could see my doctor pal reach quietly for his calculator. We both agreed we were looking for a tick, but the good doctor informed me that actually a tick need not be enlarged with blood in order to be harmful; all it needs is to be attached. Well, this changed everything and I went back to my patient for a closer inspection. Trying to find a tick on a dog's body is like trying to find a parking spot downtown 10 minutes before you're due in court. But find the little rascal I did and I picked him off and flushed his paralyzing little butt down the toilet. Within an hour, TD was up and about, crashing into the priceless antiques and expensive furniture which decorated our lovely bunkhouse.

I phoned my good old doctor buddy to inform him of the good news and make him an offer to buy him a beer which I had no intention of keeping. I kind of wanted to gloat a bit on this one as I had gotten away with a freebie over the phone this time, but he wasn't too worried. After all, Ticker was young yet and there'd be lots of opportunity down the road for the good doctor to capitalize on my "investment." And other vets were to get their chance also. Ticker went to see several different ones during his action-packed life. Where I happened to be working at the time or the severity of the injury dictated which vet in which town he was taken to. Dogfights were usually the worst for causing injuries. Anytime you have five guys with two dogs each living in the same camp you're going to have dogfights.

Ticker's worst dogfight-related injury was when two dogs ganged up on him and he had one testicle badly damaged. The nearest vet quickly fixed that problem. Many times the injuries would be minor, and small jobs such as stitches could be handled by us since we all had the necessary medical supplies to perform minor surgery on cattle.

Most of us that worked dogs realized that they needed to be cared for properly, so they could in turn, do their jobs. If you ever got your hands on a good one, the amount of work he saved you was well worth the trouble the dog caused. With Ticker, though, it seemed that most of the trouble he got us into didn't have much to do at all with work.

I had taken some time off that summer to visit my friend Rooster out in Alberta. It was early in the afternoon when I finally arrived in High River, the town my pal called home. I had been on the road for several hours that day and was getting a bit hungry, so I pulled into the parking lot of a local Kentucky Fried Chicken joint. I parked my white pick-up about ten cars from the glass front of the building and hopped out. As I walked towards the front doors, the aroma of scrumptious fried chicken beckoned me. Apparently it must have beckoned Ticker as well because he jumped out of the back of the truck and trotted up beside me, licking his chops.

"Ticker, for shit's sake, go get in the truck," I demanded. I vaguely recalled some obscure law that dogs were not allowed to dine with humans in this part of the country. He turned and skulked back to the vehicle and before my disbelieving eyes he stopped, not behind my old white truck, but behind the brand new white Cadillac parked beside it. In slow motion, I stretched out my hand.

"Noooo." Too late. He had made his mistake already and sprung up from the hot pavement and onto the car hood. Young dogs will make this boo-boo sometimes, especially with a vehicle of the same color. Once he was almost up on the car and was able to have a good look around, he realized that he had the wrong outfit. As I held my hands over my ears, I watched him as he let his body slide off the front of the car with all ten toenails making a deafening screech down the hand-rubbed paint job of the gleaming white Cadillac.

"Holy Shit," I whispered to myself. Immediately I turned around to face the huge glass windows of the fried chicken outlet. Of all the people staring at us from behind the smoked glass, one stood out distinctly.

There he was, a short bald man with a white short sleeved shirt and black tie. His eyes were riveted to mine and his hands were clutching violently at his throat. He was swaying to and fro and pointing wildly in my direction, all the while spitting chicken chunks and gasping for air.

Slowly I took two steps backward, then turned and dove for my truck. Ticker was already seated and in a gear-clashing cloud of burning rubber we peeled out of the parking lot and away from the sleepy little town as fast as we could, leaving our baldheaded Cadillac owner to dislodge the chicken bone stuck in his throat as best he could. I felt badly about this unfortunate incident but was confident that anyone who could afford a new Cadillac would be wise enough to get the best possible insurance package available to protect his beautiful car.

Just before my summer vacation ended, I decided to go out to Vancouver Island with some buddies of mine to a team-roping. We had a couple of horses with us in a long four-horse trailer. On our way back inland, we decided to stop at the huge International Air Show at Abbotsford, BC. The line-up to get in to see this thing was unbelievable and before we could change our minds, we were boxed in. As we slowly crept along we had lots of time to do the necessary arithmetic needed to calculate that the cost of the air show per person added up to three times as much money as we three cowboys possessed at that moment. It became evident that two of us were going to have to pull a fast one and hide in the horse trailer until we got past the heavily guarded front gates. So under the premise of "checking the horses," me and my accomplice, Perkins, exited the pick-up and made our way slowly back to the horse trailer. Tickerdog sat comfortably in the back of the truck looking all around at the cars that had us hemmed in on both sides, front and back.

"Excuse me, just going to check our horses." "Pardon me, ma'am, we gotta check these horses," we lied to one and all as we eased our way past car mirrors and in through the side door of the trailer.

Once inside, Perkins began to comment on how hot it was in there and how slow the line was moving. Perkins was a big, powerful guy with a heart of gold, direct from the BC backwoods. We gave him his nickname Perkins because he reminded us of the deputy on the old *Sheriff Lobo* show.

As Perkins and I sweated quietly, our outfit drew up to within twenty-five feet of the main gates. All at once there was an earth-shattering roar as two F-16's flew over us at about a hundred feet. For me and Perkins inside that horse trailer, it sounded like 200 Jamaican steel drum players were using the trailer to practice on. With his eyes still crossed, Perkins glanced out the window just in time to see poor

Tickerdog, scared plumb out of his wits, bail over the edge of the truck box and rim out into the traffic jam. Before I could react, Perkins, who had a soft spot for little Tickerdog, stumbled out of the trailer after him and into broad daylight, not ten feet from two very shocked and grim-looking security guards.

As Ticker ran off through the crowd, Perkins stomped his big old foot and put his huge hands on his hips.

"Aw, Ticker, ya blew our cover," he wailed as both he and I were apprehended and duly prosecuted to the full extent of the law. Our driver pleaded no knowledge of us or anything to do with us and promptly sprinted after Ticker, catching up to him huddled under a mini-van full of screaming kids.

We simply told the security guard that we were checking our horses and, after a lengthy shakedown, came up with the money necessary for our admittance, mostly in nickels and dimes stuck between the seat and in the ashtray of our truck.

In order to keep the line moving, we were sent hastily through and told in no uncertain terms to behave as though we were in the real world.

We agreed to this and piled back into the truck to enjoy what was left of the air show in total humiliation.

I N THE MIDDLE OF SUMMER 1985, me and a few
cowboy pals were invited to an afternoon pool party at
the home of an executive friend. Their gorgeous
ranch-style house was perched on a sagebrush-covered hill
overlooking the spectacular scenery west of Kamloops, BC.
We were living the good life that hot afternoon as we sat in
the sun, our pearly white bodies reflecting ultraviolet rays
wildly in all directions. No worries, though, there was
nobody there to impress but each other anyway, and each of
us was just as pale and skinny as the next guy.

Then, SHE walked out. Through the sliding glass door
she came in her blue bikini. I sat there with my mouth open
as this angel glided by in front of us, pausing briefly to
sweetly say hello. She had a paperback novel and suntan
lotion with her, and with the poise and dignity of a debu-
tante, she sauntered over to a chaise lounge at the edge of
the pool to lie down. As she did so, the lounge collapsed in
a heap of twisted aluminum. Us boys just stared in horror
as she hit the deck with a mighty CRASH! You could have
heard a pin drop. A lesser gal would have burst into tears
and ran back into the house in humiliation. Not this one

though, and in spite of being embarrassed half to death in front of five strangers, she calmly arose, pieced her deck chair back together again as best she could, and lay back down as if nothing had happened.

This behavior under such circumstances impressed the heck out of me, and I knew I would have to get a closer look at this lovely blonde creature with so much class.

She apparently was a friend of the host and this was why she was at this afternoon party. Her name was Christine and she drove an older pick-up truck. A pick-up truck! That was it! That was how I was gonna get my foot in the door.

The first chance I got I faked being interested in her useless truck. I figured all I gotta do is mention stuff like piston rings and spark plugs and wham!, the trap would be sprung and she'd be all mine.

And that's exactly what happened, except worse. You see, I'd never been in love with a real woman before and I really wasn't prepared. I thought that when you were smitten by the love bug, it was like getting shot with an arrow or something. Boom, it was over and you move onto bigger and better things like mortgages and diapers and the like. She would be there whenever I needed her, and my present devil-may-care lifestyle would not suffer at all.

Could I have been further from the truth? Probably not. What really happened was not at all what I expected. After I saw this gal a couple of times, I started to get this weird feeling like someone was pouring gallons of warm syrup over my head. It would kind of ooze down my neck and over my shoulders. It felt pretty good, but I didn't really want it to be there. Within a few days I was completely covered in the stuff and there was no way to get it off of me. Eventually, I just resigned myself to the fact that I was to be coated in this goo for the rest of my life and I may as well get used to it. If my soul mate felt this romantic about love, she never told me about it. I could only assume it was equally as wonderful for her, and several weeks later we were inseparable pals.

I was quite busy during those first weeks so we only really had time for one real honest date, so to speak. It started off quite informal. I phoned to say I had to take an irrigation pump into town for repairs and would she meet me for lunch. She said that would be swell, so we had a bite to eat together. TD came along for the ride and he didn't seem to care one way or the other as long as it didn't get out of hand.

After lunch, a little business, then some shopping. Later on, a couple of drinks in a quiet lounge and then off to every girl's dream dinner at Pizza Hut. After dinner, we had the rest of our pizza boxed for later. To the movies was our next stop and when we finally found a parking space, we were faced with a dilemma. I had not expected our date to go this far but we were having such a good time that Tickerdog was just gonna have to get comfortable and wait this one out. We bedded him down in the cab of the truck. But what to do with our pizza? If we left it in the front with him, surely he would devour it before we even got into the theatre. So we had no choice but to put the pizza in the back. When we returned from the movie, there was TD snoring it up on the seat of the truck, but some bum stole our pizza! That's what you get for parking so close to the train tracks.

We had a memorable date anyhow and this led to a full-fledged wedding by the time Christmas rolled around.

Shortly after we were married, Chris and I left BC for a job at the BAR TH ranch in eastern Alberta. Luckily she had the same wanderlust as I did. Her whole life had been an experience at the very least. Christine was born and raised in Las Vegas, Nevada and she spent her youth with her family in a host of locations, including California and Washington. After graduating from high school in Atlanta Georgia, she flew directly back to her grandparents' home in Las Vegas and began working backstage at the Stardust Hotel on the strip. This gal was smart, tough and pretty. What the hell was she doing up here with me everyone asked. Maybe she had a thing for Canadian guys in long underwear. I would never know for sure. But here she was, and she appeared to like me so I didn't push it any further.

On the negative side of things, she did own a very independent cat. Try as I may, I could not convince her to unload this dopey furball. Anytime I suggested selling it or trying to give it away, I would be chastised for my insensitivity. Consequently, we spent a few tense days moving that winter with all four of us crammed into the front of the truck. For Ticker to be locked up in such close confines with a cat and a strange woman who seemed to be moving in on his turf must have been agonizing.

During our move to Alberta, Ticker also made another enemy. It was just before Christmas and we drove for one day with Puck following in his truck. He was going our direction anyway to spend the holidays with his folks north of Calgary. After a day of driving, we stopped for the night in Revelstoke and all three of us split a motel room. Someone from Puck's family had sent him a care package earlier that week and in it were a dozen homemade butter tarts. Puck guarded these tarts like they were the Holy Grail, opening the box every so often to look at them and count them and savour their sweet aroma. He even ate one or two, and when we stopped for the night, he came over to my side of the truck and offered me and Chris a tart. That is a single, solitary tart to split between us. We felt honoured indeed to have been given one of the precious tarts which must have been irreplaceable. After sharing our tart and admiring the rest that were tucked snugly in the little box, we got to the business of unloading night bags, bedrolls and shaving gear. In all the commotion, I sinned greatly by setting the box of succulent tarts down on the dash of our truck.

After all was unloaded, and Ticker was tended to and bedded down inside the cab of our truck, we humans retired for the night.

Morning came fast, and for Puck, the first hunger of the day with it. Being a single cowboy and blissfully unaware of the four basic food groups, his mind instantly locked onto the buttertarts for breakfast. Buttertarts. Where were those darn buttertarts?

Right then for me, my stomach was not feeling hunger. Oh no, it was feeling that same feeling you get when you put what's left of a month's wages on the horse that has just come in dead last.

I slowly drew back the curtain of our dingy room. There, not three feet in front of us was the mangled box and crumbs of Puck's priceless buttertarts, strewn wildly across the dash of our truck. There were no survivors.

As Puck began to rhythmically hyperventilate, Ticker sat up and looked back at us from the relative safety of his truck seat. He had a content look on his face like he had just been handed a cheque for $10,000 and was looking around for someone to thank.

Because it was the Christmas season and there was a lady present, Puck took this major setback like a man. But if left to his own devices, I'm sure he would have yanked Ticker out of that truck by his neck and thrown him off the nearby bridge and onto the frozen Columbia River below.

CHRIS SURE WAS a good little cowboy's wife. She always made me breakfast and never threw any boxes away. Why, this whole husband-wife thing would have been perfect if it wasn't for her useless cat. Belina was the goddamn queen of everything. Who would own a cat named Belina anyway. Christine would explain quietly time after time to me, "you don't own a cat, they choose you." She would cap this sweet little statement off with a ballerina motion and a smug smile. This went a long way towards explaining why it was so hard to get rid of the little hairball. Belina really did choose Chris too, by jumping into her truck one hot night in Vegas. There are people on the run all over in Las Vegas, scurrying here, scuttling there, looking over their shoulders. It probably wasn't that much different in the cat world, so when Belina spotted Chris at a gas station she just bailed in to get away from whatever was closing in on her and they had been laminated together since that special night.

Sometimes me and Ticker could see Belina through the screen door in the kitchen as we sat out on the porch after supper. Her Royal Highness purred and smiled with half closed eyes as Chris prepared her a special dinner. Ticker would just stare through the screen and tremble. All cats affected him this way but Belina was becoming a serious threat to his mental health. I could hear him thinking something like: "I hate cats. Why don't I just go in there and . . ."

I sat on the porch with my head in my hands in deep thought.

"If something happens to the cat and it's even the least bit suspicious, you and me are gonna be bed buddies for a shittin' long time," I finally proclaimed.

Meanwhile back at the Nicola Ranch just outside Merritt BC, Stan Jacobs had been offered the position of cowboss and he readily accepted. Everyone knew he'd do a fine job and that's exactly what he went and did. I knew it would be a helluva place to work so I pestered him from our home in Alberta until he caved in one day in June of '86 and hired me back as cowboy number ZERO. This of course meant that I had to get all the gates, jingle the horses and they would feed me on the back steps of the cookhouse. Sounded good to me so eventually I informed Christine of our impending re-location and she quietly started loading boxes. The best wedding present that a cowboy could ever get would be a case of heavy duty packing tape and a dozen felt tip markers.

I then waltzed across the Bar TH yard and with hat in hand broke the news to John Gattey, the ranch manager and part of the family that owned the place. "Dammit, O'Byrne, I just finished writing out a big list of shitty things for you to do for the next three weeks," John complained. John and his wife Cindy had become our friends during the time we spent at Bar TH. I was sorry that the big outfit cowboying was not yet out of my system.

We headed west at the end of August. There was soon to be a third O'Byrne and everything was perking along quite nicely. Chris had a half miserable trip as any expectant mom would and judging from the staring and trembling going on in the cab of that truck, Ticker's journey was unpleasant as well.

We were down to driving Chris's old 1969 GMC four-wheel drive that she had brought up from Vegas. My old truck had blown up sometime back. This truck of hers was built like a tank. It also sounded like one and was almost as cool in the cab as one would be in August out on the Great Plains. Our trip took us west through Edmonton and as we approached the impressive little town of Edson clouds of blue-black smoke came pouring out of the starboard engine, enveloping both sides of the highway in a dangerous fog. We limped in on what little power we had and pulled behind Earl's Garage. Earl or somebody that looked like an Earl came out and said, "Problems?" He had the same tone of voice as a veterinarian and a tingle ran down my spine and directly into my right hip pocket.

I explained our crisis and he said, "Tell you what, let's hook 'er up and we'll see what's goin' on." When this was completed he switched on the little monitor. It immediately came to life and displayed four big bleeps and two itty bitty bleeps.

"Oh, I see," I lied, feigning knowledge of engines. "Two cylinders aren't firing." As the shop filled with high octane smoke Earl coughed once and spat a line between his two front teeth.

"Uh, mister, them's the good ones," and he slapped my shoulder in a most sympathetic way. Chris and the critters bailed out and went off somewhere to breathe and Earl disappeared into the parts department, leaving me alone to ponder whether this was a normal life I was experiencing or something unique. Earl returned pretty quick, replaced all six spark plug wires and turned the big computer on. I fired up the truck and the little monitor beamed its approval, six itty bitty bleeps just bleeping all over the screen. Earl charged me a fraction of what his excellent service was worth and I located my healthy family sitting under a tree out back. Off we went, west, towards Nicola Ranch. Earl waved at us then wiped his hands on a rag and walked back into his garage.

I started work on the 3rd of September and things were pretty quiet. Me and Stan knew this old ranch pretty well but I needed a refresher course on the back country. I had spent most of my previous time at Nicola either in the low country or over in Voght Valley with Bob Munsey. No worries, though, and I was enjoying getting reacquainted with the place.

One day in the late fall, I was out re-riding a piece of country. Everything was fairly quiet and as I trotted along some old cow trail with Ticker way up ahead of me, a coyote appeared out of nowhere. Then two, then three. It was very rare this time of year for coyotes to come in this close, but before I could give it any more thought, they jumped poor old Tickerdog and were pulling him in about four different directions. I was packing a gun with me at the time but I couldn't shoot blindly into this dog pack, so I bailed off my horse and tied him to a tree. I broke off a green cottonwood snag and went wading into the fracas just a-swinging.

I was batting about .900 but these suckers weren't gonna let go that easily. It was almost like they had something personal against Tickerdog and had been trying to find him for six weeks. Now that they got him they were gonna make him pay. I don't know, maybe TD slept with one of their sisters or something. He wasn't above that kind of behavior. But I believe in a fair trial, so I just kept swinging and hitting till they let him alone. As I stood there over my terrified hound dog, the coyotes circled us and barked and hissed. Then one by one they gave up and skulked off into the dark bush, leaving me and TD scratching our heads wondering what the heck we'd ever done to them.

Fall works progressed and one bright morning as me and Ticker were bringing some cows and calves down the Monck Park Road on the west edge of Nicola Lake towards the ranch, he stepped on a piece of glass. This severed a main artery in his front leg down by his foot. Blood was flowing like whiskey at an Irish funeral. I tied my hanky around it to try and get it to stop but no way. It was just gushing out all over the place. How much blood can one of these little dogs hold, I asked myself. If I didn't do something soon he was gonna check out on me. I applied pressure directly to the artery for 20 seconds at a time so I could control the bleeding. But we were still 10 miles from town and the nearest vet.

The road we were on was lonely but not totally abandoned. A car came by right about then and I flagged it down. I asked the driver to go down to the ranch which was only five miles away and tell my wife to get up here as soon as she could with the truck. He sped off and pretty quick Chris showed up. We made a pressure bandage for him and loaded him up. Chris took him quickly into town where the local vet did an excellent job of reattaching the artery.

A couple of weeks later Ticker was back to work. He limped on that leg for awhile but eventually recovered 100% and was ready for more.

The next month it was back to the vet again. He had punctured a fetlock. He probably staked it out on a nail or something. Chris doctored him for a few days with ointment and fresh wraps. A week later it was back to work.

In the spring of 1987 we were running a few cows through the chute to give them some vaccine to prevent E. Coli Scours in the newborn calves. They hadn't calved yet and by giving them this vaccination 30 days or so before they were due, the immunities in the vaccine would be transferred directly to the fetus through the bloodstream.

As usual, there were men and horses and dogs all over doing their various jobs to keep the show rolling. Ticker was working on the plank runway which runs the full length of the lead-in chute. He would lean over and nip at the cows to keep them moving along. As we were all pretty busy and not paying much attention, him and the other dogs were mostly left on their own as long as they were not stirring up the pot.

The work was going smoothly when suddenly the air was pierced by dog yelps. We ran back down the runway to find Tickerdog hanging upside down off the end of the runway, hung up by one hind leg. His foot had slipped between a space in the runway planks and he fell off the edge.

Dog's bones are like chicken bones. There's not a lot there. Yet broken bones in these cowdogs are rare. But this time we thought for sure his leg was busted. We gently lifted him out of there and set him down on the ground. We couldn't tell if his leg was broke or not, so I hauled him over to Christine back at the house. She took him into town where the local vet checked him out.

He had done quite a bit of damage to his stifle joint, equivalent to the knee of his hind leg, having crushed the joint and the pad between it.

He was out for several weeks with this injury. If it did not heal on its own, he would need surgery to repair it. Luckily for us and our bank account, he healed just fine and six weeks later it was back to work as usual.

The other men and women that worked their dogs steady in rough country like this were always having to doctor them for minor or major afflictions so Chris and I did not feel lonely. Ticker's medical history was not uncommon amongst his peers.

1

THE SUMMER OF 1987 was a good one for us. Chris and I were busy showing off our baby boy, Mark. He showed up in January of that year, and we were getting pretty used to having him around.

Ticker was in his prime. At first he ignored Mark as nothing more than a noisy toy that sooner or later we were gonna take back. But after a few encounters on the living room rug, they discovered one another and soon became fast friends.

Stan had his hands full as cowboss of the outfit. A few years back he married a wonderful gal named Shirley and the two of them were busy starting up a family of their own. Stan was pretty much his happy-go-lucky self, stuffing his mouth with snoose every so often and stomping all over the ranch, looking for wrongs to be righted. But the outfit was in financial problems, making it difficult for him to keep the ball rolling.

His time spent trying to run this cow outfit with absolutely no capital taught him valuable lessons for the future. He learned how to do the job with what he had. Resourceful Planning, they call it now. There are many men in our business who do not know the value of the hard-earned dollar. Big businesses are forged and destroyed on small decisions. When you are broke and still operating, you learn to be very frugal with any money that does come your way, and you learn to make do with the materials and equipment you have on hand.

Every ranch has a dump, or boneyard, we call them. Along with all the dead critters which show up from time to time, any old machinery, lumber and miscellaneous parts were taken there for indefinite storage. We spent many hours on that outfit sorting through the boneyard for hidden treasures. After all, the price was right.

We were leaving the ranch one Sunday afternoon heading to cow camp about 15 miles up the mountain. A couple of the boys had rimmed out already with the cavvy of about 15 or so horses. Christine and I and our baby boy Mark were seated amongst a large pile of camp goods in the cowboy crummie. A crummie is about what it sounds like. Basically it is a four-wheel drive pick-up with a crew cab or four doors with two bench seats.

Stan was our chauffeur that afternoon. Our ranch crummie was an ancient Ford with a gray primer paint job. It had a massive black "roo bar" on the front and was affectionately dubbed "The Old Gray Mare."

Stan and the ranch mechanic had made a pet project out of keeping the Old Gray Mare on her feet. They did this almost impossible task with little or no budget allowed to them. On this day, she was running in tip-top shape, raring to go like a sled dog on the run home.

In an ozone destroying cloud of blue smoke, we were off. As we chugged our way to the top of the mountain, our conversation was light. Chris was with us in Stan's employ as camp cook. We brought Mark along to serve as her alarm clock. Also, he was supposed to keep her occupied in her spare time. After all, a cook only has to work a few hours each day. Breakfast at 4 a.m. and supper at 4 p.m. The rest of the day was theirs. In this camp, things weren't too bad at all. No power meant not having to change any bothersome light bulbs, and the nearest water was 300 yards down the road in the bottom of a draw. So Chris didn't have to worry about atrophy of the muscles setting in while she relaxed all day and waited for us to return to camp.

This being her first cooking job, me and Stan damn near had her convinced of these lies when all at once—"KAPOW"—and the Old Gray Mare sputtered to a halt. Stan and I got out to survey the damage. We opened the hood and hummed and hawed a bit. I said it was this and he said it was that and Mark woke up and wanted to eat. Here we were, broke down on an extremely seldom-used trail on the side of a mountain on a Sunday afternoon with no one back at the ranch who could help us. Mark was screaming for supper and Christine didn't have any way to warm it up, so she tried to persuade him to eat cold pablum. He was christened to cowboy life that day. Rule #72 in the cowboy handbook: sometimes you're gonna hafta eat your pablum cold. But that doesn't mean you have to like it and judging by all his caterwauling he wasn't impressed.

Chris was trying hard to calm the baby; Stan was stomping around cussing and kicking tires, the dogs were in the back of the truck up to their ears in the month's groceries, and I was lying in the soft grass on the hillside, enjoying the beautiful view because everybody knew that I wasn't trained as a mechanic and I would just be in the way. I was a specialty man and would be willing to answer any "cow" questions if anybody had any.

All at once Stan declared, "That's it! I've had it! I know what we're gonna call this place. We're gonna call it the Dead Mechanic's Trail!"

With that he set himself to work under the hood with all the furor and commitment of ten Russian ballerinas. The new name definitely spoke for itself because me and Chris believed that any mechanic within twenty miles was not safe around here with Stan in his present capacity. So, we let him bang away under the hood, stopping every so often for a chew. I pulled off my high-topped Austin Halls and peeled away my aromatic socks. As I lay there wiggling my toes in the cool grass I tried to resume my secret plans to take over Western Canada while the baby cried and Chris and Stan fussed. Down through the trees off the side of the mountain I could see part of the Nicola Ranch headquarters and most of the valley leading into Merritt. "Silly little people," I thought to myself, "why couldn't they see I was a man of action." I must have dozed off because I was awakened by a loud CLANG. "Vapour lock," Stan declared, as he shut the hood down so hard it rattled both of Mark's teeth.

"Wake up, asshole, let's git." I assumed he was addressing me although I knew not where the harsh tone came from. He cranked 'er over, we all piled in, counted the dogs and off we went, sputtering and chugging our way to camp.

A few months at camp was enough for me so in September I decided to expand my horizons a bit and I pulled the pin. Stan was not the least bit surprised. Anyone who had ever hired or re-hired me was pretty used to it by now. Usually I'd hang around an outfit till the shoes on my horses started to rattle loose, then pull out to avoid having to reset them.

A lot of guys would move around the country but few could keep up to me in my single days. This was my fifth time back to this particular outfit. Sometimes I stayed six weeks and sometimes I stayed 16 months.

Now that I was married, it slowed me down a bit, made me more hesitant. I thought back to the fall of 1983 when Puck pulled up to our bunkhouse at Nicola one evening after supper. With a huge carefree grin, he announced that he had quit at Douglas Lake and was heading for Oregon to find work, and this would be good-bye. As all the boys swarmed around for handshakes and some last minute trading, I sat back in silent thought. Then I jumped to my feet and declared, "Good-bye my ass, I'm coming with you." As the boys stood staring, I disappeared into the bunkhouse and returned with my bedroll and warbag. I fired them into the back of Puck's truck and we headed for the barn to get my rigging. In a few short moments we were history, leaving our cowboy buddies blubbering and sputtering back on the porch.

But that was back in the bad old days, and now that Chris and Mark were my travelling companions I was a little less impulsive. Neither of them seemed to care much which way the wind blew as long as we were together and happy and making a decent living.

So when I announced that there was a job at Baird's Feedlot a couple miles down the road, the packing began.

This particular feedlot offered quite a few advantages to me personally. It was small enough that I could learn the pen riding end of it as well as the feeding and machinery end. I would be home every night, which can actually benefit a marriage in some cases. But best of all I would be back working with Bob Munsey again. Bob had been working there for a year or two. This would be a definite kick in the butt and as it turned out it was one of the best periods I ever had to learn from him.

Around about May of 1988, Chris, Mark and I took a week off. We left old Tickerdog with strict instructions to take good care of Bob and the feedlot while we went away on a little vacation to visit Christine's family in Vegas. He took his responsibilities quite seriously and set about immediately to make certain that no one tampered with the garbage or the dead pit. He had been spending most of the first two days splitting his time between these two duties when he was summoned by Bob to help pull a pen of steers. Bob's constant companion these days was a solid brown female kelpie named Duffer. She was another giveaway that Bob snagged a year or so beforehand from Stan. As can be expected, Duffer was a very happy-go-lucky cowdog, seldom disciplined, and heard every word Bob said to her but didn't listen to any of it. I believe she would politely dismiss Bob's words as advice and not actual commands. At any rate, they seemed to complement one another and today they called upon Tickerdog to be their guest in a pen pull. Ticker and Duffer worked well together just like Fred and Ginger. So off they went, on a hot, hot spring day.

The steers knew something was up the minute the gang entered the pen. Heads were up and tails too, and as Bob and the hounds worked their way to the back of the pen, the rodeo was on. These big old soggy steers had been kinda bored lately and today they were gonna have some fun.

The dogs began to bark, Bob began to yodel and the steers began to play. Some ran out the open gate, some bucked and kicked, some ran to the back of the pen, and one tried to jump on Bob. Two began to butt heads and the dogs peeled another one out and ran him head on into the feed-bunk. One jumped into the water tank, and those that ran out the gate before, came charging back into the pen.

All hell broke loose. Bob was trying to get his horse to be three places at once, and the dogs were doing their best to turn the cattle around without getting stomped on. The dust was boiling, cuss words were flying and big fat steers were galloping in all directions. Then the dogs did the unthinkable. When Bob tells the story, this is the part where his eyes go glazed and his voice gets sorta low and mean.

He was in perhaps the biggest fiasco of the decade, and right when he needed them the most, those faithful idiots who were supposed to be helping him just quit him cold. As steers danced and jeered all around him, Bob stood and stared in mortification. Ticker and Duffer had simply had enough playtime and thinking as one just plain stopped everything they were doing and strolled over to the water tank. As the turbulent episode continued around them, they lapped their fill of cool water and lay down in it to refresh themselves. They felt no shame, no humiliation. Oh, no, not them. They had it so easy for so long here at the feedlot, that they just couldn't see what all the fuss was about. What's the big deal. If you couldn't get them today, you'd get them tomorrow. It's not like they're going anywhere. Besides, neither one of them had been on a long circle in quite a while and they were both pretty much out of shape.

Bob stared at them jaw hanging down to the saddle-horn. He had never seen cowdogs quit in the middle of a good storm, even free dogs. And so the story ended with Ticker and Duffer, eyes closed, lying in the water tank enjoying their bath with Bob trying hard to believe what was happening, and 300 big fat steers laughing so hard that some of them fell down and had to be helped back up.

THE BAIRD FAMILY OWNED the feedlot and ran a pretty good show. I learned a lot about the proper way to feed cattle for a profit. Although I only stayed there nine months before my feet began to itch again, I enjoyed every minute of it. There were still some things out there that I had to do, and cowboying wasn't completely out of my system yet. Being two years my junior and only 125 pounds, Chris didn't have the courage to speak against me. Poor Chris, all she ever wanted was a little house with a white picket fence and curtains, but she failed to convey her true sentiments because she didn't want to hold me back. So this time she willingly came along for what was to become a true adventure.

1988 was a year of change for a lot of cowhands in the area. Stan had moved on to the Douglas Lake Cattle Company, eventually to become the cowboss later that year. He hired me in July to cowboy full-time. Me and the family were sent to Chapperon Ranch, one of the four divisions of the main ranch. This division ran a bunch of cows and an even bigger bunch of yearlings.

Chapperon was a bit isolated compared to some places.

It was 10 miles from the main headquarters and a good 65 miles from the nearest town. There was no phone but we had a two-way radio that connected us to the main headquarters. We had electricity, and the loggers would plow the roads all winter long so we were in good shape.

Within several months there were some personnel changes, resulting in an opening at Chapperon as foreman. I promptly submitted my application and was hired for the job, mainly because everyone else had left and I was all alone. I was the King of Nothing but who cared? I certainly didn't. Besides, I had a crew already. In addition to Ticker-dog, I now had another faithful kelpie to call my own.

Christine decided I'd need another dog since we were back on the big outfits again. So for my birthday, she arranged to purchase one and have it delivered. The gal that owned the dogs came out to the ranch one afternoon, and after greetings all around she opened up the back of the vehicle and out poured six roly-poly brown kelpie pups. Then they were gone. Six Tasmanian devils disappeared in six different directions. It took us quite awhile to gather them up again. We chased and coaxed and threatened and pleaded. Finally we had them all cornered where I could take a look at them. I chose the runt of the litter, a chocolate brown female who I named Sammy. She was a cute little affair that just would not stop squirming around.

The lady who owned the batch gave me a deal. If I took Sammy, she'd give me another little brown female to try out, and if I liked her, we would work out a deal later. I agreed to that so before I could change my mind, she drove out of the yard. The first thing we did was fix a place for them in the basement. This worked out fine until one day Chris came upstairs to find me.

"Come down to the basement with me. I want to show you something," she said with a hint of mischief.

Down the stairs we went, down to the basement, down into the biggest mess I'd ever seen up to that point in my life. It looked like a marshmallow factory blew up. The Tasmanian devils had cornered and attacked a big old foam mattress that was stored down there, leaving meatball-sized chunks of it absolutely everywhere. And in the middle of it all were two innocent cherubs, tails wagging and proud as hell.

The offenders were immediately put on probation with no hope of appeal. I thought I had a lot of patience when it came to animals, but when these two jerks were together, it was too much for me. Anytime I let them off their chain to run around, that's exactly what they did. Run around. The whole ranch, that is. You just couldn't control them. I tried letting them go at different times, but the one that had to stay home would raise such a ruckus that it wasn't worth it. So I had no choice but to break up this little partnership or risk losing my mental health. I kept Sammy and sent the other one back.

While Sam was busy growing up into a mature, out-of-control kelpie dog, me and Ticker had some serious work to do. While we were punching cows all over Douglas Lake Ranch, we got a chance to see some terrific country.

One day in the fall of '88, a bunch of us ended up back in the Hathume Lake area of the country. As we trotted along over this big open logged-off flat, I couldn't help but notice the high population of fat groundhogs living in the area. There were slash piles all over and at least five groundhogs were living in each one. As we meandered through this chunk of country, the dogs were way out ahead of us having their own fun. You see, as far as a cowdog is concerned, a groundhog was put on this earth entirely for the dog's amusement. They're meant for chasing, and that's just what our dogs were doing that day. The groundhogs know how to play the game too. They will stand out on a rock or log about 25 centimeters from the front door to their hole and tease the dogs. They will razz and torment them with high pitched chirps until a dog makes his charge. Then 'plook,' into the hole the groundhog goes, leaving the attacking dog scratching and whining with his nose jammed in right up to the eyeballs in vain pursuit. And so it goes and has gone for centuries and will continue as long as there are dogs and groundhogs around to pester them.

Ticker was right in the middle of the fun. It was every dog and groundhog for himself. As we trotted along laughing and enjoying the show, there was a sudden frantic disturbance up ahead. It all happened in an instant. Ticker-dog was half lying there frozen in his tracks about two feet from one of the little varmint's holes. He was kind of crouching down and it looked like he had something there in front of him. Could he have actually caught one of the little buggers? Usually they're pretty quick, and to tell you the truth, I'd never seen a dog catch one before in about 65,000 attempts.

As we rode up for a closer look, we saw that sure as hell he did have one. I guess these hogs were so far back in the bush that they never got much company. All of a sudden, six or eight of us show up like a blizzard and catch them suntanning. There they were, all flustered and out of shape and two pounds overweight (this is plenty for a groundhog). It therefore would be possible for one of our lean mean dogs to have surprised a plump one and nabbed him. But wait a minute. As I got closer I began to see just who had who.

There was Tickerdog, frozen stiff, eyes as big as hubcaps, and a big fat furious groundhog hanging by his teeth off of poor TD's cheek. He had caught himself a dog and he wasn't going to give him up.

God, we all bust out laughing so hard I could hardly get anyone to hold my horse. TD was so glad to see me. He just looked up at me as if to say, "Get it off!"

I put on a couple pairs of leather gloves and got me a little stick and tried to persuade Mr. Groundhog to let go of the death grip he had on this poor dog. "No frickin' way," says he, "not till everyone sees what I've got." By this time all dogs and other groundhogs had ceased activities and were watching the show. I managed to convince the little varmint to put the dog down, which he did. The little rascal then dusted himself off, stomped over to his hole and in he went. As we gathered up our belongings and Ticker collected himself, our groundhog stayed just out of sight in the safety of his hideaway, cussing Tickerdog up and down in an indignant tone of voice.

We mounted up again and headed off, with TD nursing his cheek like he'd just come back from the dentist. The rest of the dogs scattered once again in hot pursuit of the elusive groundhog. But not Ticker. Nope, there'd be no more groundhogs for him. He was much too humiliated by having been the first big bad cowdog in the history of mankind to ever be caught by one.

WINTER WAS IN FULL SWING now, and all the cattle were home and happy on the feed grounds. In our end of the universe, we move the big cowherds around to wherever the hay happens to be stacked. When you're talking a couple thousand cows, it doesn't take long for them to run through a thousand tons of hay. Sometimes the fields where the hay is put up and stacked may be five or ten miles apart. So it is not uncommon to be moving 500 cows down the road on any given day.

Usually this happens to come around when the weather is downright frosty. This particular day was such a day, about 35 below with a bone-chilling fog that made it feel like the North Pole on Pluto. As we left the security and warmth of the house and trotted out on the hay meadow to move yet another bunch of cows, conversations amongst the three or four of us cowhands turned to office jobs. Usually every year we discuss how good it would be to have one right about now. Of course not one of us would last in an office long enough to finish a cup of coffee let alone assume a career.

As usual, TD was way up ahead of us trotting along on

a cow trail in the snow. He trotted right out onto slick ice covering a beaver dam, not a care in the world. KERSPLASH! Through the ice he went, plumb out of sight. I saw the whole thing because I was 50 feet behind him. Up he bobbed like a bar of soap and he did the dog paddle to the edge of the ice where he tried to pull himself out of the water.

"Come on, Tickerdog, you can do it!"

Furiously he clawed at the ice, trying to lift himself up out of the freezing cold water. "Come on, TD, come on!"

It's no use, he started to go back under. The look on his face spelled imminent doom.

"For shit's sake, how much do I have to go through for this frickin' dog, anyway?" I definitely did not want to do it and I held out as long as I could. Finally I bailed off my horse, plugged my nose, yelled "Geronimo," and jumped in. Luckily the water was only up to my armpits. Or maybe I was in and out so fast that I never touched bottom. But it was cold. Very cold. Extremely cold for me, in fact. I grabbed Dingus by the scruff of his paltry neck and fired him out of the water and into a snow bank.

Then I trudged back to my horse, mounted up, told the guys I'd be back in a minute and headed for the house. Luckily we were only a mile from the main yard.

By the time I got to the house, my clothes were froze stiff. I thought I was gonna break the legs off my jeans going down the stairs into the basement. Christine met me and played the role of the concerned wife. Ticker got the day off, thawing out in the living room by the fire and I got dried off and a new set of clothes. Now that I was refreshed and wide awake, I kissed my lovely wife adios. I set off to enjoy my day, content in the knowledge that as I froze my butt off, my idiot dog was probably lying in my recliner back at the house while Christine hand-fed him Milkbones.

Around the late spring of 1989, Sammy was beginning to accompany me on some long circles. She was gung-ho from day one, getting bigger and stronger all the time. She was still completely out of control and now that she had a little age on her was about the fastest little critter on four legs I'd ever seen. Sammy always struck me as being half wild. If she was ever hungry and feeding time did not come fast enough for her, she would go off in search of a bite to eat at the local dead pit. Yet she exhibited some of the most loving and affectionate characteristics of any dog I've ever seen. She got to be extremely protective of Mark and she just wiggled her little butt off whenever he called her "Sammydog" in his high-pitched little voice.

If she would have been lucky enough to have had a good dogman to train her, she would have been a fine dog. But as it was, she was stuck with me. In her exuberance, many mistakes were made, some forgivable and others not so forgivable. Many times I would have strangled her if I could have caught her. But I kept telling myself, "It'll take years to train this dog, but when she's five years old, look out." That's what I kept telling all the guys, too, who were helping me clean up all the cattle wrecks she caused. I'm sure they wanted to strangle her sometimes too.

I finally had my chance to tune Sammy in. I was counting about 600 yearlings through a gate up at the Norfolk Division one day. Norfolk is a Douglas Lake hay meadow camp situated nine miles east of Chapperon. The guys were stringing them through for me and Sammy was in there screwing everything up. About halfway through I was so mad I called a halt to the whole dismal affair. This particular count had to be dead on exact and to the last animal. I didn't need her messing me up because these yearlings were going out for the summer and we only had this one last chance to count them for the books. I dismounted and persuaded her to come up to me. She usually didn't do this; she was too smart. But today she did. The method taught to me to discipline a working dog was to twist their ear until they felt a little pain, then back off.

So I gingerly reached down to get ahold of Sammy's ear. I gave it a gentle twist, thereby (in theory) sending an instant message deep into her psyche to decipher right from wrong and never do anything bad again, forevermore.

Good on the blackboard, but not in reality as cute and cuddly Sammy chomped onto my hand sending me into a blood spurting, screaming chicken dance in front of about 300 bewildered yearlings who were waiting patiently to be counted through the gate.

Grumbling like a madman under my breath about how much one man should have to endure at the hands of his own cowdogs, I wrapped my hand with an old snotrag that had been flattened into the back pocket of my jeans for what may have been years. As I mounted my horse, I looked down at little "Precious," who looked up at me with an expression as if to say, "What did you think was gonna happen?"

I finished counting the cattle. We closed the gate and headed for home, my day completely ruined. I learned something about Sammy that day. I never tried to physically discipline her again after that, except for a couple of times when I made sure I used a long stick.

I figured by summertime and turnout I would lay off Tickerdog and camp on Sammy. I figured if I could wear her out with lots of long circles, maybe she'd slow down and quit zinging around so much. Who knows, maybe she'd learn something and the guys wouldn't be mad at me all the time. So Ticker got his pink slip and I concentrated on wearing down the Tasmanian devil.

TD did not take the retirement well at all. He was getting kind of lame in one front foot, so I had thought he'd appreciate the lay-off. I would leave him in the house until us cowboys were gone. About an hour later, Chris would let him go outside. He would stomp over to the barn, sit down in a pout and wail away making sure everyone within a five-mile radius knew that I had left without him. Then after 10 minutes of this, he would get mad. He would sit there in front of the barn all day long, just steaming. And all day long he would bark. Just one bark at a time, exactly nine seconds apart, until me and the boys returned home from work.

The next day we'd get up and do it all over again, me to work, and him to the barn to pout. This went on for about three weeks. I didn't mind a bit but because the house was right beside the barn, poor Christine was beginning to show some wear. To her and Mark, this nine-second bark must have been something like the Chinese water torture—drip, drip, drip.

I noticed something was a bit off when she insisted on putting the dirty laundry in the fridge and started wearing her jeans backwards. When I inquired as to why the odd behavior, she stared blankly at me and explained the events of the past three weeks while I was away at work.

I immediately rectified the problem by putting Tickerdog back on the payroll making him a very grateful hound indeed.

Instantly the ranch was restored to its original peace and quiet and I had my old Chrissy back.

EVERY SEPTEMBER for many years the cow country around Kamloops would come alive for a few weeks. The Panorama Cattle Sale is the highlight of the fall. This is a special week long affair with cattle sales every day. Most of the critters sold at this time are grass-fat yearlings. The big outfits have spent many weeks gathering up and sorting their yearlings and the country takes on an almost festive air. The week generally starts with a sale or two in Kamloops or wherever. Then the cattle buyers, along with the ever present entourage of Lookee-Lou's, proceed out of town for cattle sales on the ranches in the area. Most of these ranches will have too many cattle to make it feasible to truck them all into the sale yards in town and sort them there. The easiest way to get it done is to bring the auctioneer with his portable microphone and the half a dozen qualified buyers out to the ranch. The ranch owner or manager and crew will have the critters that are to be sold already sorted and penned before anyone even gets there. Pretty quick, cars and trucks will start to trickle into the yard and before you know it, a full-fledged crowd has gathered and an auction has begun.

So it was that September, like it had been last September and the ones before that. Us cowhands at Douglas Lake had spent a couple of weeks trying to bang our yearlings out of the timber. The guys on the south end had a lot more critters to deal with than we did. But I think we might have had more fun with ours. They had around 2500 steers to gather up out of pleasant, grassy country. We had 600 spinny yearling heifers to get hold of in some pretty depressing bush.

Our crew consisted of myself, a couple of other cowboys and our assorted dogs. We were left alone for about 10 days to do the best that we could to find as many heifers as possible. No one in management expected us to get many more than about 80% of them captured. The job was not an easy one for two reasons. Mid-September in the BC Interior can be very mild and pleasant some years. If this is the case, as it was this particular year, cattle—especially yearlings—will be scattered out in small groups of 10 to 40 head or so. When cowboys jump a little mob of these critters on a nice September morning, more often than not they will just plain scatter like quail. The "head for home" signal that Mother Nature has so thoughtfully supplied these animals with is activated only at cooler temperatures. As the weather turns cold and the grass goes brown, the cattle will instinctively begin to think about leaving the bush and heading for a more hospitable environment such as a nice hay meadow, but since the weather was so mild for our gather, the cattle were reluctant to leave.

The other reason our job was so tough was that we were dealing with yearling heifers that had been turned out in the bush for three months. Sometimes heifers will react quite differently to some situations than steers or older cows.

They may have a tendency to be a little more flighty and will often chose escape mode over submission.

So here we were, us cowboys and cowdogs faced with a nice tidy little challenge. We thought it over for a bit, then decided amongst ourselves how we were gonna get this done. We would use the tried and true hold-up method.

Ticker was sound again and in his prime. Sammy was hell on wheels and really coming along nicely. She was making a pretty fair head dog and we were really gonna need her now.

One of my partners was Trevor Thibeault who had been punching cows with me at Chapperon for a while. He had two wonderful black and white border collies. Trevor had married his high school sweetheart when they were both young and spent most of his life punching cows on the big outfits in the sagebrush west of Kamloops. He had a black moustache and was built like Arnold Schwartzenegger's little brother. Trevor was at the top of the heap as a big outfit cowboy and wasn't scared of anything. I was about five years older than him, he being in his mid-twenties and because of this, I made him do all the dirty work any chance I got, citing a vague age clause from the 'International Law.' He let me get away with this most times but was content with the knowledge he could tear off one of my arms and beat me with it like a rented mule. We worked well together and once, after he tried to teach me how to crack his bull whip, he even visited me in the hospital where they had sewed my ear back on. Trevor's delicate collie bitch was named Tammy and she was fine-tuned like a vintage Jaguar. Spuddy was his big mean stud dog and I was scared shitless of him on the ground. The prick knew it too and made me beg for mercy every time he caught me afoot out in the yard somewhere.

The other fellow who was with us at the time had a pooch too, so about the 8th of September we set off in search of our cattle. The area that we had turned these heifers out into was perhaps seven miles long and three or four miles wide. It consisted of a complex system of good and bad roads and trails connecting various hot country (where cattle are), cold country (where cattle ain't), lakes and meadows. It was fenced almost all the way around but the backside went up into some pretty rough timber. The cattle rarely went that far due to the poor feed up there. Our plan was to concentrate on one given area each day and try to work together as a team rather than tackle the whole piece and be spread out far apart. We decided to set up our plan so that each man would have a specific job to do. Two of the men would gather small sections of country simultaneously and bring any cattle they found back to the third man. The third man would act as the hold-up man and his duties would be to stop and hold the cattle that had been given to him by the others.

The first little bunch to be jumped in the morning of each day were usually the most important to get stopped. They would serve as the nucleus of the day's gather and they had to be allowed to calm down so that one man could quietly handle them. As one can imagine, that first bunch always acted like a group of chorus girls that had just had their dressing room invaded by half a dozen photographers. They would be very flighty and nervous and we would just have to sit on our horses with them in the center and let them relax. After fifteen to twenty minutes, you could see them visibly calm down. Then they would be left in the care of the hold-up man and the work would begin. Before the others left to find more critters, a predetermined rodear spot would be decided upon. The hold-up man would then ease his cattle down the trail towards that spot and the others would disappear into the bush only to surface half an hour or so later at the rendezvous point with more critters. The dogs helped out immensely to contain these cattle.

Of course all this worked fine for the most part but having pulled my shift as hold-up man a time or two, I can remember witnessing some odd and unusual sights while waiting in some meadow with fifty yearlings while the cowboys banged around in the bush. At times not a word would be heard as a steady stream of bewildered cattle would trickle out of the bush smack dab into the middle of the rodear. Some cowhand may have spooked them up a mile or so back but maybe he never even saw them. Of course, the cowboy responsible for that side of the gather would always come up a hero by faking his knowledge of the circumstances and leading everyone to believe that he had indeed jumped those animals and boogered them down the trail to the rodear grounds before going off in search of more.

One day shortly before noon a half-dozen wild-eyed heifers came boiling out of the bush and right into the small rodear Sammydog and I were holding. With Spuddy and Trevor in hot pursuit, the whole bloody works smoked right on through my sleepy little herd and out the other side disappearing into the bush in a barking, bawling, cussing tangle. The hold-up cattle looked strangely at one another as the crashing and screaming grew distant and faded away until all fell silent. I took a chew from my tobacco pouch and my horse fixed his ears intently on the spot where the intruders had re-entered the thick bush. The hold-up cattle settled once more and some bedded back down. I sat there on my horse and relaxed with my arms folded for perhaps 20 minutes when finally six heifers with tongues hanging out marched solemnly out of the timber and joined the rodear. Right on their heels like prison guards appeared a very hot and tired Spuddy along with Trevor, who by now was much more familiar with that particular portion of the BC Interior than anyone else alive.

The distance between hold-up spots was rarely farther than half a mile. This meant a lot of starting and stopping the hold-up. By the end of the day the heifers would be very easy to handle and as wilder ones were thrown in with the rest, they would surrender to the calming effect of the whole herd. None of these cattle were even close to being wild anyway; they were just a little hard to stop at first. This routine went on day after day and we would trade off who was to be hold-up man. The dogs just loved all this great yearling work, and it was one of the more memorable endeavors I've ever seen to demonstrate what good dogs can do to help out if given the chance to learn through the years. Our dogs were always lucky enough to have all sorts of this type of work all year around. There is never a shortage of cattle to move on a big outfit.

A week or so of this and then we went back into the whole country and straggled up for a day or two. Sale day was closing in on us so we pulled out with what we had, which is about what the ranch managers expected us to get and what they'd got in any previous years.

Douglas Lake Ranch had yearlings coming out of their ears and it took fifteen cowboys three days to sort them all and get them graded for the sale. We had our 560 or so heifers waiting in a large fenced field about five miles up the road from English Bridge and soon it was our turn to bring them down to be graded. Stan sent a couple of cowboys to give us a hand to accomplish this, and with Trevor and I proudly out on point, we delivered the cattle triumphantly to the Bridge like explorers home from a three-year trip to Antarctica. At the end of the day after our cattle were put away, and we headed quickly back to Chapperon to jingle up our best bridle horses. The next day was Sale Day and the whole damn valley and then some would arrive at noon like lemmings to partake in the Douglas Lake Ranch's sumptuous beef barbecue lunch prepared by the Ranch Ladies' Club.

The big day arrived in splendid fall form and us cowboys started out early. The bosses had a strict and calculated schedule to follow in getting each classification of cattle penned in their respective pens before the noon barbecue broke out. The crowds began to arrive about 11:00 in the morning and a carnival-like atmosphere began to develop. We just barely got the cattle penned in time to grab a quick beef-on-a-bun and a beer amid the laughing, gossiping groups of friends and neighbours.

Precisely at 1:00 pm the auctioneer announced through his scratchy megaphone that the auction would commence immediately. Everyone threw down their paper plates and crammed down the first cattle alley to watch the show. There were perhaps two hundred people there in all: craning, climbing and stretching to get a look at the action as the auctioneer, perched wobbly up on top of a wooden gate, tried to stay balanced and hold his dented red megaphone at the same time. Desperately at times he coaxed and squeezed bids out of the six or so qualified buyers and with a nod or a wink, they would respond.

"SOLD," he declared with a booming voice. He climbed down from the gate as the crowd shuffled down the alleyway towards the next pen. It didn't take long to sell 3000 head of cattle in this manner and before we knew it, she was all over. Almost immediately us cowboys were directed to start weighing some loads out for trucks that were already waiting at the loading chute. As usually happens at these occasions, it was a job in itself to get people out of the way and gates set up and scales balanced. There were brand inspectors and cattle buyers and film crews scattered all over. There were lost kids and runaway dogs and old retired cowboys watching the show. We pulled about 60 big soggy Hereford steers and punched them down the alley towards the weigh scale.

Ticker was right in there, doing his best to get them moving when all at once– WHACK!– a big fat steer kicked him right square in the forehead and it sounded like Babe Ruth knocked one out of the ballpark. He dropped like a brick and lay there totally unconscious. As I stood beside him and wondered if he was dead or not, I really didn't have a lot of time to ponder this question because a wall of fat thousand-pound steers were descending rapidly upon us. I grabbed him by the scruff of his neck and fired his limp body out of the alley and then clawed my way out of there in order to save myself. The steers stampeded on down the alleyway as I inspected my lifeless hound. He just kind of lay there like a rag doll and I didn't really know what I could do for him. I kinda kicked at him a bit with the toe of my boot and asked him if he was OK. Soon enough one eye opened and he slowly lifted his head. He had this dreamy grin smeared all over his face and I felt it best that he just lay there for awhile.

I really felt sorry for him that time because I couldn't help thinking how ironic it was that his great big reward for the work he had done in the last few weeks was a good swift kick in the head. But after he came around, he really didn't seem to mind about the poor treatment. After all, he had started his working life in much the same manner and was really getting pretty used to the routine by now.

FALL WORKS HAD SNUCK UP and surprised us again as usual. Before we realized what had happened we were well into November and busy preg-checking the cowherd.

Stan had set it up so that 800-head cowherds were relayed to the ranch headquarters from their respective summer ranges. Us guys from Chapperon would be present each day to help as best we could, and as each cowherd was walked down and delivered to us—this usually took the other crew a couple of days—we would gather them into the pens on the third day and strip the calves. As the calves were being weaned, a couple of men would sort through them in a separate pen and split the steers from the heifers. The calves would move on to other pens during the day to be sorted for size or breed type, and eventually all the different cuts would be sent to their respective pens in the feedlot to be fed, watered and bedded down.

The fresh-weaned cows would be penned separately overnight without any feed but with access to water in preparation for the veterinarians pregnancy test the next day. Some vets like them to be penned this way because it makes it easier to do a rectal preg check when the cow is empty of manure and the stomach is not full of feed and pressing up against the other internal organs.

The fourth day would be totally taken from dawn till dusk with preg checking and giving all the pregnant cows their shots. On that day as we accomplished this, the other crew would be delivering us another 800-head cowherd and we would repeat the process until the whole 6000 head were done. Of course it is much more complicated to orchestrate than that, and about this time of year Stan's vocabulary would be reduced to a few grunts and one syllable words. His motto soon became "Be Prepared For Anything," and likely this was the reason that he survived these fun-filled weeks.

One bright and chipper day we were well into a morning's preg checking down at English Bridge just a few miles from headquarters. Everyone had their job to do and once everyone got into the routine of things, it usually went quite smooth. There would be a man running the hydraulic headgate and doing any necessary work on the front end of the cow, such as trimming horns or checking eartags. A couple of guys were on the other side of the chute to give shots, the veterinarian was there to do the coveted rectal examination job, and a couple of guys brought the cows up the chute. Our crew was rounded out with a lovely records person to keep track of what cows were pregnant and whatever—this usually being a cowboy's wife who had been volunteered for the job. As always, the dogs had their own particular departments. Some days Sammy would specialize in stealing lunches and skulk around all morning like a hyena waiting by a waterhole for a sick or injured gazelle. Some dogs would lay around and wait for any poor animal which have chosen to linger a little too long in the chute. They would then lunge in and give the cow a little incentive to rim out.

Today Tickerdog decided to help push the cows from the back. The "Blue Goose" was our massive steel hydraulic chute setup christened as such because of its royal blue paint job. At the front was the chute itself in which a cow could be properly restrained and worked on. A long narrow alleyway behind the chute was just wide enough for a mature cow to walk into and it was known as the "snake." The snake was long enough to hold about eight cows and was arranged in a semicircle. As the cows passed through it single file a spring-loaded stopper would pop out behind them and prevent the cow from backing up. The stoppers were designed to work much the same as a subway turnstile and the snake of the Blue Goose had three of them in place. Each time the stopper popped out behind a cow it left a square opening in the side of the snake and Ticker must have seen this as an opportunity to nip at a cow. All at once he cried out in severe pain. We had been pumping cows out of the chute like they were the little donuts at the Calgary Stampede midway but the production line ground instantly to a halt.

He had stuffed his beak in one of those little square holes in the chute at the exact same instant that an eleven hundred pound cow lurched ahead. The spring loaded stopper was pushed back up into the little square hole and Tickerdog's snout was pinched severely. The top of it was cut clean through to the bone and one canine tooth was broken off about halfway down with the rest of it split down the middle, exposing the nerve. Ooh, that must have hurt. Luckily, Dr. Paul Christianson was standing not 15 feet away and he happened to be one of the best vets in the business. Removing the hockey helmet he always wore while preg checking in order to protect his head and face from miscellaneous flying material, he examined his patient more closely.

He declared the wound not too bad, but the dental work was a mess. He referred me to a specialist down in Oliver that did all kinds of small animal dentistry. Sheesh, now I have to pay for a root canal for this ding-dong. What next? I hated to ask that because I remember asking myself that the last time. Next thing the son of a bitch is gonna need bifocals or something.

Anyway I got a special appointment with this doctor and took TD down there the next day. The good doctor did an absolutely splendid job of fixing the tooth. He did the root canal, smoothed all the rough edges down and capped it. It truly was lovely and I paid for every bit of it. I did not think of whether this friggin' dog was worth it anymore. You see, I was well past the point of no return and had way too much money invested in his well-being to ever turn back now.

Tickerdog at Voght Valley, Nicola Ranch.

Tim, Chris and Mark on the edge of Churn Creek, Gang Ranch.

Williams Meadow Camp, Gang Ranch.

Larry Ramstad on Archie branding at Cotton Corrals, Gang Ranch.

Moving calves across the Fraser River Bridge from Gang Ranch.

Tim and Stan went to check out the back country camps of Gang Ranch in early fall. This is Stan topping out on Dash Plateau overlooking Relay Valley.

Puck working with a young horse at Raspberry Creek, Douglas Lake.

Mark's first day of correspondence school, the wagon, Williams Meadow Camp, the Gang Ranch.

Tim and Mark at Williams Meadow, Gang Ranch.

Sammy and Tickerdog relaxing at Gang Ranch.

I WASN'T THE ONLY ONE having all the fun with cowdogs around that time period. Some of my friends were entangled just as much as I was with their own canine partners.

When Puck and Stan and I were punching cows together a few years before, Puck had a good old half kelpie dog he called Boss. Now old Bossdog was quite a character, a very friendly, low-key kind of dog.

The first time I ever laid eyes on him he was just a little pup at the Nicola Ranch. We were all milling about outside the Voght Valley bunkhouse one evening after supper, roping the dummy and telling lies. Somebody threw this pup the bone out of our pot roast. This was a big old round cow bone about three inches in diameter. The other dogs never had a chance. Little Bossdog just bailed right in and proceeded to crunch that big old bone into little pieces and swallowed them while the other dogs stared in shock.

He grew into one big tough son of a gun, but always retained his gentle, almost bashful nature with people. Puck's pet name for Boss was "Bosshdog" for some reason and that's what he always called him. When Puck issued those standard voice commands "Bosshdog, bring him," old Bossdog became a cow's worst nightmare. He absolutely loved to scare the living hell out of cows, especially bulls. Badass bulls were a specialty of his, and he took pride in his ability to fine-tune them. God help the insolent bull that tried to hit the thick stuff on Puck and old Bossdog. "Bosshdog, bring him outa there," was all that needed to be said. Boss was gone like a rocket and pretty quick the timber would start to rattle. The sound of growling beast and bawling bull would be heard, and then the bush would explode like a beaver dam blowing up with willows and brush flying in all directions. The hunter and the hunted would appear as a blur and soon the renegade animal was back in the herd with Boss trotting happily back to join his partner and get on with the day. Puck always got a chuckle out of Boss when he put on a "logging" demonstration using one of the ranch bulls.

This backfired once though, and damn near got Puck a couple of broken bones. He was loafing around outside the Voght Valley bunkhouse one afternoon. Stan was just coming in and he had a black bull that he'd been wrestling with all day. Stan had gone a different route that morning, hence the reason he was riding in late. He had to bring that bull right through the yard and in front of the bunkhouse to get him into the corrals. Of course Puck was standing right there and he was gonna help by maybe blocking a hole somewhere and haze him into the corrals. We all know that this rarely works, but for some reason we do it anyway. Cattle that are worked all the time on horseback generally flip out when folks start to crowd them too much afoot. That's just what this idiot bull did. He took one look at Puck standing there and he plumb quit the country. But Puck wasn't the least bit worried because lying over there on the porch as calm and collected as a funeral director was good old Bossdog. All he's gotta do is say the word, and say it he does.

"Bring him, Bosshdog, bring him."

Boss knew very well that Puck and Stan could not do this job without his expert assistance.

He launched himself from that wooden porch like an F14 Tomcat off the deck of the *U.S.S. Enterprise*. Six leopard leaps and he was just a-chewing on that old bull's juicy hocks. Stan and Puck just held their ground and stared in awe as Bossdog furiously worked to bend that old bull in a huge arc through the scrawny trees on the edge of the road. The poor bull, fearing extinction of his own personal body, ran blindly through the brush with his head bent back, bawling wildly and demolishing everything in his path.

Puck's command vocabulary for Bossdog was quite simplistic. "Bring him" in this case proved to be an unwise choice because that's what Bossdog was doing right now. He was bringing a 2000-pound bull straight toward skinny little Puck standing on foot in the middle of the road, barely casting a shadow. Puck was but a mere orange cone on the big highway as the semi, loaded with lead pipe, closed in on the poor lad. There was very little he could do but close his eyes and hold his breath until impact. The bull neither saw nor felt poor Puck as he steam-rolled over him and continued down the road, with Bossdog frantically in pursuit.

"OOOOOO, Bosshdog," Puck moaned from a crumpled position on the gravel.

Puck used to stutter a bit before that episode, but he didn't anymore, and pretty quick he was all healed up and him and Bossdog were ready once again to terrorize the neighbourhood.

Me and Puck and our two useless dogs punched a lot of cattle together over the years. But for reasons known only to them, Ticker and Bossdog were to be mortal enemies throughout their entire lives. We'd see them work side by side to literally destroy a badass bull or keep a cowherd together and then at the end of the day be so choked up at one another that they could barely eat. For me this shall remain one of the great mysteries of life.

Puck, Stan and I were now reunited once more at Douglas Lake Ranch almost ten years since we blew into the country. Stan was the cowboss, me the Chapperon foreman and Puck the Hathume foreman. This outfit was pretty big and we didn't get to cowboy much with one another but we got enough in to keep it interesting. Stan was busy training a new male kelpie that he'd got ahold of. His name was Charley and he was a big gangly kind of dog.

Douglas Lake Ranch had built their silage pit on the edge of some fenced hay meadows not far from the English Bridge cattle facility. Essentially the pit was built into a hillside, about 200 feet long and maybe 20 feet high along the walls. It was lined entirely with concrete and measured 80 feet wide, big enough for a semi to manouver around in.

One day in late spring when the pit was almost empty of silage, a couple of cows had wandered off to the nearby meadow and were making a nuisance of themselves in the area. Stan and Charley took it upon themselves to return the cows to their rightful place and began an earnest game of "ring around the silage pit" with the cattle in the lead. Stan and Charley went this way and the cows went that way. Cowboy and dog swapped ends and mounted a counter offensive only to have their plans foiled by the devious cows. In desperation Stan knew he was going to have to split his team up and send Charley way round to the other side of the pit to block the cows' attempt at a getaway or else this nonsense was going to go on all day. This would never do because Stan's hair appointment was scheduled for 3:00 that afternoon and if he was late due to these rude cows it would be just dreadful. So seizing the moment, Stan gave the command "Go 'way around, Charley."

What he meant was "go the easy way around." But nope, not Charley. He was a kelpie dog and he wasn't gonna take the easy way around. He took off like his tail was on fire and bailed off the edge of the pit into nothing but thin air. There happened to be a truck driver unloading a truck-load of grain, shoveling away, minding his own business in the bottom of the pit. All at once an unidentified flying brown creature narrowly missed him and landed, KERSPLAT on the concrete beside the truck, scaring the living daylights out of the poor unsuspecting man. Charley rolled on the pavement a couple of times and then he was up and gone again, not missing a lick. There would be plenty of time to heal up later, but right now Stan wanted him to be somewhere and that's where he was gonna go. Both Stan and Charley got off lucky that time, but the truck driver was probably a bit jumpy for a couple of days afterward.

During the spring of one year at Chapperon, there happened to be a young fellow working with me and Trevor by the name of Corey Newton whom we labelled Newt after the *Lonesome Dove* character. He had a collie dog named Lefty. Poor Lefty used to have two nuts but some-how one of them was extracted leaving only the left one, thus giving cause for his imaginative name. Me and Newt, Ticker and Lefty were trotting back to the barn one after-noon after we were done work. We were heading for our usual shallow crossing on Chapperon Creek, but the spring waters had made it very fast and treacherous for the dogs. As we crossed our horses, Ticker swam it with no problem, but Lefty was swept away in the fast muddy water. In an instant the dog's head was completely under water and his limp body was swept down the creek and out of our view.

Newt rode his horse across the creek, bailed off on the opposite side and ran as fast as he could to try and intercept his poor dog. In the meantime, I built a loop in my rope and loped down my side of the creek hoping to snag the dog if he surfaced. Soon both of us came to where the fence crossed the creek. It was log fence on both sides right up to the edge and then it was just a rail suspended across the creek wired to some old sheep wire. We almost beat Lefty to the fenceline and in one final attempt to grab him, Newt bailed into the frigid and fast moving water. Poor Lefty was sucked under and disappeared in the torrent.

But we had bigger problems. Poor Newt had not only missed saving his dog by inches, but now he himself was trapped in the icy, swift current. It ran so strong that his skinny body was pinned up against that old rail and he couldn't go under it or over it because of the huge tangle of sheep wire. Worse yet, that old rotten rail was beginning to break under all the weight.

If it broke with him out there like that and he was hung up by his spurs in all that wire in the rushing water, that boy was gonna be in some serious trouble.

I bailed off my horse and tied my rope to a tree. It must have been getting kind of serious because I don't tie a knot in my rope for anybody! I threw him the other end hoping he would catch it, but he couldn't take his arms off the rail or he would be sucked under. I thought maybe I could drag him out myself, so a big GERONIMO and in I went. I extremely underestimated the power of that creek because right now, instead of one hopeless fool up to his armpits in fast water, there were two. I guess what happened next would best be described as a clawing, pushing, pulling, cussing, let's get the hell out of here scramble for the bank before this rail gives out. Before you know it, we were both lying there huffing and puffing and froze up good.

As we gathered up our gear and horses, who stumbles out of the thick tangle from down the creek but good old Lefty, nine tenths drowned and not looking near as fluffy as before he went swimming. He dragged his waterlogged bones up to his cowboy buddy and collapsed beside him.

Like a bad hangover, hypothermia set in on all three of us so we figured we'd better keep going. Besides, what if the big bossman caught us loafing around on such a splendid afternoon as this. Newt and Lefty came slowly to life and I untied the knots in my precious 60-footer. As we mounted up and headed off down the creek bank, I noticed Ticker-dog sitting impatiently on the other side, wondering just what the hell the hold-up was.

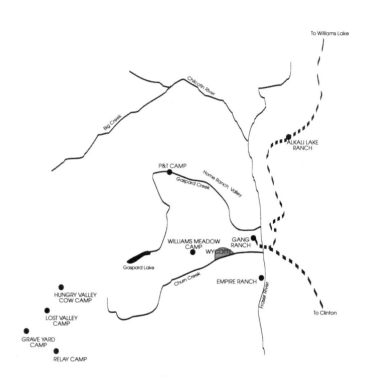

GANG RANCH AREA OF BC

IF ANYONE EVEN MENTIONED the Gang Ranch to us young cowboys we'd get so excited we could scarcely breathe. The Gang to us was the ultimate "out west" adventure. This huge outfit was nestled innocently enough on the west banks of the Fraser River in the South Chilcotins. Strange and awesome things happened in the Chilcotins. Things that didn't happen anywhere else happened in the Chilcotins on a regular basis. Just the thought that one of these things might actually happen to us would be our beckoning.

The Gang Ranch was going through some changes in the first part of 1991. The ranch itself appeared to be somewhat lax about the process, having seen this type of transfiguration many times before in its hundred-year history. Larry Ramstad was the general manager of the Gang at this point. He had been manager of Quilchena Cattle Co. back down in the Nicola Valley and it was there that I had been in his employ, so to speak. Larry and I had always got along. He was a cowboy, cowman and general manager all rolled into one neat happy-go-lucky package. He was in need of a new cowboss so I foolhardily offered my services, complete with my wife's services too, whether she was aware of this or not. I must have been the sole applicant for the job so he slapped my name on the payroll as cowboss, but first I had to quit my present job.

It was late one evening that winter when I tracked Stan down at Douglas Lake headquarters. He was tromping around in the snow outside the poorly-lit salt shed.

"Hi," I said, my voice devoid of confidence. He just stared at me. "Guess what, I'm going to the Gang Ranch," I squeaked like a gopher who wasn't quite sure if he should run out on the highway or not.

Stan spit a wad on the sparkling snow. "Go for it," he declared and stuck out his big paw for me to shake. Having me quit on him for the third or fourth time sure was doing a lot to mellow the man out.

Bob Munsey had managed the cow end of the Gang Ranch back in the mid-seventies when it was much bigger. Some major pieces of real estate had since been sold off. He always had a soft spot for the place and was excited to see me go up and try my luck. It was his wise advice that eventually helped me through many a pickle I found myself in.

When I arrived at the end of January, Larry filled me in on the sorry state of affairs he had to deal with. The ranch was in need of some major tender love and care in every department except bookkeeping and the main cookhouse. The cows were old and used up, the spring country had long since been grazed off and there wasn't a camp on the whole place fit for a vagrant packrat. We had lots of horses, some of them were even broke. It's a good thing too because transportation in the form of a reliable truck and trailer was non-existent. We had a one-ton red Ford with a horse box on the back but one day somebody's horse smashed out the rotten side of the box and ended its usefulness.

The Gang Ranch had every conceivable type of country on it somewhere. There were steep scary river breaks and high sagebrush, mid-elevation bush and high alpine meadows. There wasn't too much to the west of us but 300 miles of mountains before you hit the Pacific Ocean.

Through the first year the crew and I pretty much punched cows and fixed fence. We saw a lot of country off the back of a horse since our red Ford was usually broke down somewhere. It gave up on us one time not one hundred yards from our remote Williams Meadow Camp. We were so busy and so pissed off about this that we were going to set the piece of junk on fire. But it was ten feet away from the main gate into the horse pasture and to burn a truck this close to a fenceline was sheer lunacy. After the fire burned itself out we'd probably have to replace a bunch of fence that had been barbecued, and to a cowboy this was not acceptable. So we left it there as a statement or maybe even an artistic expression of the crew's sentiments and by the time we got around to fixing it several weeks later a pack rat had moved in and selfishly claimed it as his own.

The ranch had an old covered sheep wagon on rubber tires dubbed "Home Sweet Home" by our many predecessors. We finally located this mythical monstrosity broke down and abandoned in a cottonwood patch in secluded Home Ranch valley. With great engineering skill we retrieved it from its lonely exile and rebuilt it into a cook wagon that was clean, outfitted with a stove, sink and all the amenities, and we finished it off with a gleaming coat of new thick red paint. A better cook wagon could not be found in all the provinces of Canada. Most of the camps were so overrun with pack rats that it was a pleasure to have a place to keep our cook stuff clean as we frequently moved around. Its only flaw was the ceiling. It must have been designed by leprechauns because it was only five and a half feet tall on the inside. The cook, therefore, had to remain slightly slumped over all day while preparing our meals and cleaning up. Christine spent a lot of her time cooking on it when we pulled it out during the summer and fall and we became quite good at pulling camp when we had to.

One day in late fall as our wagon was situated at Williams meadow our plans changed early in the morning and I arrived back at the wagon unexpectedly about 10 o'clock. "Chris, we got a chance to pull camp RIGHT NOW and save us a day, let's do it." Long pause. Her hands were full of flour because she was rolling homemade noodles on the counter. There were two chickens stewing in the pot on the stove and a fire in the little wood heater. Mark was stacking wood outside and playing with his cat.

"Oh, OK," she said, with only minor hesitation. The boys rimmed out with the cavvy, I piled bedrolls and warbags into the back of the pick-up and hooked it up to the wagon. Chris banged everything shut inside and within half an hour we were steaming down the road to our next camp with a pot of warm chicken on the floor of the truck cab, and a long gray trail of smoke coming from the tin chimney on the wagon.

By 4:00 that afternoon we were rolled out in our new camp and sitting down to a nice plate of chicken and noodles. This is about what we had to do to get the job done and we got pretty used to it after awhile.

We had established a larger more permanent camp on the edge of the existing Pinette and Therion Logging Company camp in upper Home Ranch valley. This was now a deluxe mid-ranch camp complete with water, sewer, small horse set-up and we were connected to the P and T's generator for power. The crew was split up most of the time now, and I hired a gal named Sheila to sling hash full time for the main crew while Chris kept cooking part-time whenever she was needed. Sheila had cooked in the remote hunting camps up north where the only thing between you and a hungry grizzly were thin canvas walls of a cook tent. There weren't many surprises left for us to throw at her and she settled in quite nicely.

The dogs were happy because I needed to use them quite a bit. There were times when I wished that I would have had a half a dozen more to help us. They were in top condition because, being devoid of any reliable horse-hauling vehicle, we trotted out of camp most of the time with the dogs tagging along.

One early morning found four of us cowhands on the long trot heading down country along the top of Gaspard Creek. The boys in the other camp had punched a herd of 250 cows into the area the day before and bedded them down by a small lake. Our job was to pick up the herd, push it up the creek and past our camp and drop it at Fosberry Meadows. The other crew would drop us another herd just as they had done the day before, and we would relay these herds along like this until we had a thousand cows at Fosberry. This would take about five or six days.

It was early in the summer and we were making good time on our way to pick up our herd. We four were busy trotting along, joking and telling lies with the dogs out front as usual. It was just Ticker and Sammydog today and they were full of piss and vinegar and anxious to get where the action was.

I watched the dogs trot around the bend in the trail when suddenly in the early morning dawn a flash of pure, shiny black caught my eye in the early morning dawn. The dogs were gone like lightning. I remember turning to the cowboy who was right beside me and saying, "What the hell was that?" We could see a long ways up the trail now and were just about to shift gears from a long trot to an all-out lope when all of a sudden we caught sight of Sammydog coming back around the bend in the trail and heading down the straightaway towards us as fast as she could possibly go. Her little belly was skimming the ground and her hind legs were reaching 'way up ahead of her ears in an effort to cover some country. When this little dog throttled up, she was, without a doubt, the fastest little varmint in the Western Hemisphere. Or so I thought up until now. Coming around the bend at full lope and stretching out on the flats was a big black wolf.

Ticker was nowhere to be seen, it was just Sammy and that big old mean wolf. She was running the race for her life. Her eyes were as big around as pie plates and her tongue was dragging on the ground. The poor little thing was giving it everything she had to get back to us before this monster ate her for breakfast. If we had been another hundred yards apart she wouldn't have had a chance. That wolf was gaining on her with every sinewy, athletic movement he made. The sheer power and speed these wild buggers possess left us completely shocked. He plain and simple was out-running that little brown bullet and he looked like he wasn't even trying. As Sammy sped into the safety of our mounted ranks, the wolf caught sight of us for the first time. He never missed a lick, didn't hesitate, spook at us or even slow down. He was about fifty feet away and his ETA was 1.5 seconds. As we stood there dumbstruck like four lawn ornaments, he calmly leaned to the left a bit and banked his lithe black body off the trail, into the bush and he vanished like a ghost.

"Holy Son Of A Bitch," I screamed, and we were gone, heads down, eyes closed, crashing blindly through the bush as fast as our horses could carry us. Farther and farther we went into the dark timber, trying in vain to gain some ground to get a closer look at this magnificent animal. It was hopeless. One by one we quit the chase and circled about, cooling our horses and trying to calm ourselves down. The adrenaline had been put to the test this morning, boys, and she was working fine.

All four of us were humbled greatly by the awesome raw strength and daring of the black wolf. As we milled about trying to piece together what had happened in the last few short minutes, the wolf began to howl at us from the spooky darkness of the thick timber. He yipped and yapped, taunting and teasing us and daring us to come farther. It was so very surreal, and Sammy wasn't having any part of it. She was scared absolutely to the brink and refused to leave the security of her horseman saviors.

We turned and started to pick our way out of the bush back towards the trail. Tickerdog had followed us in and we met up with him halfway. He had chosen wisely to sit this one out and had remained hidden from sight while the whole drama was being played out. When Sammy saw him she ran up, gave him a big old sloppy kiss and damn near wagged her little tail off.

We hit the trail, picked up and delivered our little cowherd. The rest of the world never even knew what had happened to us that day. When we told Sheila our story that night after supper, she didn't bat an eyelash. All in a day's work on a big cow outfit.

Poor little Sammy was always getting into trouble with critters that made their homes in the bush. Being a full-blooded kelpie herself, she was known to display her dingo side of the family from time to time. Sammy often followed her wild instinct to fend for herself. She would leave a full bowl of food on the porch and trot merrily back to a dead cow she had seen on the way home two days earlier. Sammy was born on the planet earth and in every sense of the word she made this planet her home. She would survive quite happily indeed anywhere on the surface whether it was the Australian Outback or Hollywood and Vine. And she certainly did not see what all the fuss was about each time she randomly invaded the territory of one of Canada's indigenous species.

It was on a fine fall morning that Sammydog and I left the security of our quiet Williams meadow cowcamp and trotted out to meet the day's adventures. On a morning such as this we could only pity the rest of the common world what with their headaches and the stress of living in society. Me and Sammy's society consisted mainly of jackpines, tolerant cows, other cowboys and cowdogs. We all so busy having fun that we never got in each other's way much and it was this flippant lifestyle that made our version of society a whole bunch better than the real world's version.

We were headed out to straggle the Wycotte, one of my favorite chunks of country because it consisted mainly of grassy flats and breaks overlooking Churn Creek. The creek separated Gang Ranch from Empire Valley Ranch to the south and was not really a creek at all. It was more like a small river that would scare the dogshit out of an experienced rafter during May and June. Along the creek there were abandoned gold panning cabins and the bleached bones of dead cows and bulls rimrocked and forgotten during the winters of long ago. The cold and crystal water rushed and splashed through the narrow gorges and over boulders as big as a fire truck. On the bench above the creek a herd of bighorn sheep grazed and frolicked. Mysterious springs dribbled water in the hills above, their secret locations betrayed by swaying green aspens bunched among the jackpines. The black rotting log buildings of the old Wycotte homestead stood silent and sad in a jade-coloured draw. One rusty wheel from a baby buggy lay in the dirt as the only evidence a family had ever been here at all.

As Sammy and I swung through a section of Wycotte called Goose Lakes we found the entire area completely vacant. There wasn't even a fresh turd anywhere to be found as we made our way above the lake across an open sidehill.

As usual, little brown Samantha was out front and very much alive. Quick as a wink she was gone up the hill and into the thick timber, hot on the trail of some unidentified beast. My brain was just getting ready to send a message down to my feet to hit the spurs when out of the bush came a frantic Sammy with her tail sucked hard between her legs. Right on her ass just a swinging his paws like Sugar Ray was a big old bobcat, ears pinned flat against his head and hissing like a stepped-on snake. Poor Sammy was about ready to apologize to this mean old cat for trying to put the run on him like that. There were lots of cats back at headquarters that lived around the cookhouse but Sammy had never seen one this big and ugly. As was the established pattern by now, my little doggy was hauling her ass back to me for protection and bringing her attacker along at a high rate of speed. As soon as the cat got within 25 feet of me he swapped ends and busted back for the safety of the timber.

Most of Sammy's courage was restored and we both piled helter-skelter into the bush. We followed our cat to a large bull pine and pulled up at the bottom while he scratched and scrambled up into the branches. He yowled and glared at us much the same way a defendant would glare at the prosecuting attorney.

Wild cats are interesting creatures to watch. They are extremely rare to see, even for us cowboys who are adept at sneaking up on all sorts of wild critters and catching them in any number of embarrassing situations. Since we had this one treed, me and Sam settled in for a bit to study this elusive wonder of nature. He was awfully big and I fear he would have made julienne fries out of Sammydog if he could have caught her. After about twenty minutes of "Here kitty kitty," we pretty much had him tamed down and he did not appear quite so disgruntled. So we said our good-byes and left our pet bobcat to the safety of his perch. As we trotted merrily away we made certain to remember the spot so we could continue on with the taming of our cat if we were ever back this way again.

LOTS OF THINGS REMAIN the same throughout history and I strongly suspect Murphy's Law was well in place long before Murphy was even born. One bright fine morning after turnout was over, I was about to test the old Law to its limits.

It was a lovely Sunday morning brimming with hope of a magnificent summer's day. I hadn't seen too many of these since I came to Gang Ranch, so I was savouring every minute of it. I had turned the crew loose for the weekend, and in their excitement they had abducted Sheila and taken her with them as they left our main Pinette & Therion camp the night before. I wasn't sure if she was taken against her will or not because her screaming was drowned out by the whoops and shouts of the cowboys as the whole crazed delirious bunch roared away in a cloud of dust and barking dogs. Then the camp fell silent.

I slept soundly that night and awoke early, ready to greet the coming day. After a hearty homemade breakfast of Fruit Loops and apple juice, I saddled my shitter and lined out of camp. The plan that I had set out for myself was to straggle the narrow grassy Home Ranch valley real quick, take any cattle that I found and kick them up into the bush country past our camp. So easy, I thought, and my reward was to be two glorious fun-filled days with my lovely family who had waited patiently two weeks for my triumphant return from camp.

Ticker and Sammy were so happy that day that they could hardly stand themselves. The three of us rimmed out down the valley in unison, pathetically unaware of what the day had in store.

After a couple of hours of empty country, we jumped a little harmless Black Angus bull. What a treat, we thought. He was a two-year-old bull that had just spent his very first summer out here in the real world. He had been born on a farm and spent his first eighteen months of life tap-dancing on Farmer Brown's toes and banging heads with a dozen or so of his siblings. After we had bought him and brought him out to the ranch with a few of his buddies, we pampered them in their own separate pen for awhile. Then, in late spring we had turned him, along with his counterparts, out with the heifers to breed. Although it appeared fun at first, it soon became apparent that this was to be no picnic. Because in addition to the young naive bulls, there were also some old experienced bulls. These old experienced bulls weighed almost 2000 pounds apiece. They didn't like young naive bulls at all.

So the new kid had spent the entire breeding season getting beat up and pushed around by mean old bulls twice his size. He was beginning to feel like one of those steel balls in a pinball machine. Finally, he'd had enough and he quit the country cold, only to wind up days later in my beautiful Sunday circle.

I didn't want him there. I just wanted to do my little

circle, go back to camp with a couple of fat old cows, get rid of them, jerk my riggin', kick my horse out and head for home.

But there he was right in front of me. Ticker and Sammy saw him too and they both looked up at me hoping to share in my game plan. Before I could formulate one though, our little bull threw a "number nine" in his tail and pedalled as fast as he could off in the direction of Gaspard Creek's steep banks. Me and the dogs boiled around in an effort to thwart his attempts at escape and we managed to bend him into a small stand of cottonwoods. I could tell from the look in his eye that he planned on taking me with him if he was gonna go out in a blaze of glory. Cautiously I rode up, talking to him in a low voice. When I came within range he flipped out, put his head down and rammed me on the starboard side full throttle.

I was shocked, stunned, mortified that some scrawny, pail-bunting reject from a dairy farm would pick a fight with me. Honestly if he acted like an arsehole at this young age, imagine what havoc would be wreaked upon the ranch if he were allowed to mature into a 2400-pound bonehead with his present disposition. It was my duty to rearrange this beast's priorities from aggression to submission. Otherwise someone might get hurt if he did not learn to respect a man on horseback.

I got the OK from Tickerdog and Sammy, so down came my rope and I hung one on him. This wasn't hard to do because he had his head pressed firmly against my now bruised right leg and was rooting away like a pig after a potato. Once I had him roped and dallied, I wound my twine around the nearest cottonwood tree and worked and suckered and finally got the dink snubbed up tight to the little tree. He was kind of mad at me now, because Farmer Brown never used to do this sort of thing to him, no matter how he behaved.

I wrapped my rope off and got down from my horse. What a lovely day. I tied my horse up about twenty-five feet away and went over to a small sapling. I took out my pocketknife and cut off a switch about five feet long and an inch and a half in diameter. This guy was eyeing me up suspiciously now, and as I sauntered over in his direction he came at me with more than hate in his eyes and stretched that old nylon rope to its absolute maximum recommended limit. As he did this I reached out with my big stick and bopped him one on the end of the beak. Ooh, that didn't agree with him at all and he came at me again, eyes bulging and rope groaning. I bopped him another one on the beak.

This is a terrible but necessary method to teach a very large enraged animal to respect and not to kill a human. If bulls don't learn this at an early age, they will become uncontrollable. Mortal man has no hope against an animal that outweighs him 10 to one. The only way to be able to handle animals this large is to teach them to respect a man and not challenge him. This was what I needed to do with my badass bull. Every time he would strain against the rope and try to eliminate me, I would smack him on the noodle with my stick. Soon he would learn that it hurt a lot less if he would simply discontinue his advances toward me.

It was getting kind of tropical out by now, so I decided to take a break and shed some of my sweaty clothing. I lay down in the shade and my dogs immediately came over to play. We rolled around in the cool grass and teased one another. It seemed like such a perfect day, and it was going to be as soon as I was done tuning in my little bull.

My break was now officially over, so I picked myself up and strolled over to see how my student was making out. After another twenty minutes I had him in submission. When I walked over to his right side and laid my stick on him, he turned away from me. Same with the other side, so I thought I pretty well had him trained. Time to let him go. I'd come back some other day after he'd thought about it for a little bit. Maybe I'd bring half a dozen cows along with me to make it easier to get him out of the valley. Sometimes a badass will go a lot better if he's got a little company with him.

As I gamely reached over to pull my rope off his neck, he turned to greet me. No damn way was I gonna touch him around his head. He'd let me poke him with my stick as long as I stayed four feet away, but once I got close to his head with my hand to try to release him it was show over. I tried several different ways to get him to give me some slack to get my rope off, but to no avail.

Finally I decided to cut my rope as a last resort. I was about ready to swap ends on the old twine anyway. I thought there was no sense in cutting it 'way back there I was when I could saw away on it up close to the bull's head and not waste so much of my rope. Hiding behind the tree I deftly reached in and chose a spot about one inch from the honda just behind his left ear and as he leaned away from me, facing toward the thick timber, I gingerly sawed away. Surely I could outrun him to my nearby horse. First one strand, then two, then 'twang,' the furious beast was free. And I was exactly 25 inches away from him when he swung around, face to face with me. He gave one big snort and up the little tree I went as fast as my adrenaline could carry me. Shit, I thought I had him tuned in already. As my bewildered dogs looked on, my bull buddy was bonking his head against the tree trunk and I was clinging like a coconut to its pitiful upper branches, hoping to hell he didn't knock me out of there. Ten seconds ago I was mighty glad to have this little tree to climb, but now I was beginning to see that it wasn't much of a tree at all. It was only about 30 feet high and 10 inches in diameter at the bottom. As the mad bull did his best to log me out of there, I swayed precariously to and fro at the top of my delicate perch. "Oh tree, don't fail me now," I prayed.

I'd never thought much about this tree before or any of the trees around here for that matter. This was a high traffic area right on a main cow trail and I'd probably passed this poor little tree a hundred times before but I'd never noticed it. There were lots of trees in BC.

Now here I was, right up in the top of it, able to touch and smell it and see it up close. As my ignorant bull rooted and fussed down below, I thought about my little tree and how it started out as just a small sapling. It was probably as old as I was, this tree, perhaps even born in the same year or even the same month as me! Imagine, this noble little tree, growing and waiting all these years, just waiting for the day when I would come along and end up having to depend on it to save me. This little tree was my friend and I was never gonna forget him. But he sure was uncomfortable. There wasn't much to hang on to up there. My little tree was pretty wimpy in the branch department and I couldn't really sit down on anything lest I break it and fall out on my heinie.

After about half an hour this was beginning to get a little old. My bull wasn't leaving. He just camped out at the bottom of the tree and waited. A couple of times I figured

I'd had enough and attempted to crawl down out of there but every time I got close to the ground he'd come back to life and put me back in the tree.

I'd been up there now for about an hour. I was thoroughly disgruntled at this unfair treatment that had been thrust upon me. It was a gorgeous day. I was young, healthy and had lots to live for. I was a nice guy to some people and felt I really didn't deserve this. Here I was, stuck in a tree on a beautiful Sunday morning, birds chirping, bees buzzing and not thirty feet away lay my ever faithful houndogs, snoozing in the cool grass and dreaming of rabbits or dog chow or whatever it is dogs dream of.

I thought about the rest of the world and what they were doing. Father, mother and the children walking to church in the sunshine wearing their best clothes. Golfers out on the courses just enjoying the hell out of themselves. Young people packing frisbees and soda pop into the car and heading for the park. Nobody knew I was here and nobody much cared. It just wasn't fair. Cowboying was a terrible occupation. God, I wished I'd been accepted at the Chamberlain Academy of Accordion and Tap Dance like mom had planned. The situation was made worse by the fact that my precious tobacco pouch was peeking out of my jacket pocket, not more than a stone's throw away in my heap of discarded clothing down on the ground. Cowboys can weather pretty near any storm as long as they've got a good chew to settle their nerves. Right now I didn't have any. The pressure was starting to get to me.

Enough was enough. It was time to take matters into my own hands. "WAKE UP YOU LAZY VARMINTS," I yelled to my dogs. "BITE HIM UP, EAT HIM UP, GET ON HIM."

"Let's get this show on the road," I thought.

Ticker and Sammy were more than willing to help. I thought if the two of them can hold this clown's attention for a second, I can climb down out of here and make it to my horse before the bull has a chance to smear me out. Then I'll ride away and take the dogs with me. After he disappears, I'll ride back and get the rest of my clothes. Piece of cake.

So, as the potlickers spun the bull around in circles, I yelled "GERONIMO" and bailed out.

I fully expected to hit the dirt running and my feet and arms were doing the four-minute mile, but my body had sickeningly come to a stop just two inches from the ground. The back belt on my chinks had hung up on a short little snag and it left me swinging from that tree like a cheap set of wind chimes.

Needless to say, I was absolutely horrified. Time was of the essence now and I gathered my wits in a flash, unbuckled my leggings and fell to the ground with a thud. With no time to spare I sprang to my feet just as the bull caught sight of me out of the corner of his eye. I rather surprised my dozing horse as I untied him and clawed my way into the saddle, but now that he was awake he wasted no time in vacating the premises. Up and over the hill we went in an all-out cold-jawed runaway, me clinging to my horse's neck in my pink long johns, the bull doing his best to catch up and stomp me to death and the dogs yapping and chewing on his heels.

My poor horse was having a stress attack from being woke up that quickly and because he was running for his life, it didn't take long for us to lose our bull. We came to a gradual stop on a little hill and turned to look back. My little black bull was standing proudly with a look of total victory on his face. With one last snot-scattering snort, he turned in a huff and stomped off in the direction of the thickest timber.

Boy I sure showed him. I'll bet he won't try me again, the dink. I think the dogs were laughing at me, but I'll never know for sure.

We headed back to the scene of the crime to gather my belongings. After I pulled myself together, I turned towards camp in defeat and humiliation. I vowed to do anything within my power to avoid answering any questions on what I did that day. And from then on, anytime I happened to pass the little tree in my travels, a hint of a smile would cross my face and I would give him a subtle tip of my hat.

F ALL WORKS OF 1991 went off with all the usual hullabaloo one would expect. What with various catastrophes, some major and some minor, it all came together in normal fashion. We were trying out a few new tricks that we had thought up to improve the work and step up productivity. The dogs played a major role in getting our cattle gathered and our back country cleaned up before the snow came and shut everything down.

There must have been half a dozen good dogs on that crew at the time and Ticker and Sam were right smack in the middle of them.

Soon our work was over and our re-rides were almost finished. The cows were home, the calves were gone and the farm crew were greasing the hay feeding equipment. All the camps were closed and the crew were getting ready to spend a nice quiet winter cleaning things up and kicking back before spring rolled around again.

One crisp January day a couple of us were out riding amongst the cowherd as they were being fed their daily hay ration. We spotted some big old wolf tracks in the snow by a dead cow. The wolves hadn't killed this cow; we knew that she had died a day or two before. We weren't too concerned about the wolves disturbing the cattle at all. This particular pack that called Gang Ranch home seemed to have a routine of sorts. The year before I had come they showed up in mid-January to scavenge any dead cows that were laid to rest off the hay meadows out on the edge of the bush. They never bothered anyone, just hung around for a couple of days, ate their fill and then vanished. It was the same this winter. We saw their tracks and knew they were out there somewhere. They lived there and so did we.

A week or so later, the whole crew was up on the feed grounds for the cattle audit. This is a year-end inventory of all stock present on the ranch and all cattle must be counted down to the last cow. We would bunch each cattle group up on the feed grounds and then the boys would string them by single file and they would be counted.

We just left our last cattle group and were walking our horses back to the ranch. It was colder than a nanny's noo-noo, with ice and snow all over. About six or eight of us were coming through the last gate when we saw three wolves 'way out in the meadow up ahead. Two greys and a black one. Me and the jiggerboss roared over for a closer look. The black one quit the country and we caught the two greys out on the slick ice of the frozen hay meadow.

Our jigger screamed on by me, and his horse bailed out on the ice and went skidding right past the wolf nearest to us. The wolf just closed his eyes and held his breath as the cowboy blew on by him and went down over the bank and out of sight.

We got a good close look at our wolves, anyway, and after that episode we never gave them much thought.

A few weeks after that was Valentines Day. It was mild

and the ranch was quiet as I stepped outside that morning. I had some business in town and after I left the house, I went over to let Sammy and Ticker out of their winter dog set-up. They seemed happy that morning as I rough-housed a bit with them and turned them loose in the yard. I then jumped in my pick-up and rimmed out for town. I never saw my dogs again.

When I returned home that night, Chris informed me that they had been lounging around the patio most of the morning, and late in the afternoon before it got dark she went out to feed them and put them in the doghouse for the night. But they did not show up and she was worried. It was normal for them to take a walkabout during slow seasons like this. Boredom for active dogs must be terrible and one cannot blame them for wanting to go find a little action. Although they had always returned at night, this time they didn't.

The next day we went looking for them. Usually, working cowdogs can be found in a few obvious places. The dead pit was number one on my dogs' list so I looked there first. No sign.

I tried the cookhouse next because that was another favorite hangout of theirs. Our cook was very generous and kindhearted, and handouts to woeful-looking dogs were not out of the question. No luck.

Sometimes if you want to find the whereabouts of off-duty cowdogs, you need go no farther than the nearest pen of cattle. Often they will go and play with the critters to relieve the boredom and hone their skills. This freelancing is greatly frowned upon, especially when the unfortunate victims are horses. I checked every feeding group of cattle on the place and not one kelpie dog was to be found.

We looked in another popular trap for cowdogs, the tack room in the barn. Many times I have seen a wore-out dog crawl into a corner of a tack room after a hard day's work. Only after doors are closed, lights shut off no cowboys are headed across the yard to the cookhouse will somebody say something like, "Anybody seen my dog?" Invariably the person with the missing hound will retrace his steps to the tack room, open the door and his dog will dart out of the shadows. But when I looked in our tack room there was not a living soul.

We continued our search through the days to follow. No one on the ranch had seen them. We thought that maybe while they were out on a prowl, someone had picked them up and taken them away. It seemed unlikely that they would jump into a vehicle with a stranger, but we hoped that they were safe. So we phoned the local radio stations and put ads in the papers everywhere. We put up reward posters with their pictures on them but still we never heard a thing.

Of course there were all the usual false leads one could expect and all proved fruitless. How could they just disappear like that off the face of the earth? After a few weeks went by we began to wonder if they had wandered up country and met up with the wolves. This may have happened and if it did, there was little wonder why the dogs never returned. I have heard a few people in the country tell of dogs attacked viciously by wolves and killed. Apparently it is not uncommon in this country. I certainly did not know enough about wolves to know if this was true, but the sources of these stories were reliable folks whom I believed.

I hoped sincerely that this was not how they met their fate. It was too violent to think about and my poor dogs did not deserve that.

The land above our house was very unstable and prone to violent shifting and sloughing. This activity left deep holes and rifts at random throughout the grasslands above the ranch, some as deep as 15 feet. It was treacherous enough to travel through this country in the summer with the small holes in plain view. But to travel across it in winter with snow covering the cracks and crevices was suicidal.

Could they have wandered up into this wasteland and fallen through the thin crust of snow into a deep, lonely grave? We looked everywhere and anywhere that we could think of and as the weeks continued to stack up there was still no sign at all of my precious dogs.

Ever so slowly, like the sun setting on a cool summer evening and taking its warmth along with it, I began to see that they were gone forever and I was never going to see them again. They had been stolen from me, taken so quietly that I had not heard them go.

As spring arrived and the cowherds began their annual move towards the high country, I really began to miss my two companions.

Every creek crossing, every rodear ground, every camp had its own memory for me, some vivid and some fleeting. At times during the day I would find myself faced with a situation that I would normally send my dogs in to fix. Out of the force of a habit born almost ten years before I would catch myself calling for them to "Go get 'em. " Only silence and an empty feeling would be there now.

I was angry at them for running off on me like that. Why did they need to go anywhere? Everything was fine at home and they had all that they needed.

Chris was trying to be tough and not let their disappearance bother her too much. After all, maybe they were still alive somewhere and somebody was taking care of them. But it wasn't good enough. She missed them a lot, especially Ticker. Her and Ticker had come to an agreement of sorts ever since she had entered our dismal bachelor world. Things had been swell as far as Tickerdog was concerned, until SHE showed up. Then he started to notice that I was acting a bit sillier with each passing day until BOOM! All of a sudden she's here all the time. But as the years went by, they had turned into the best of pals. Sammy was her special gift to me and Chris had watched her grow into a cowdog. She felt privileged to have had a chance to see those remarkable dogs in action.

Mark had grown up with the dogs hanging around and they were his friends. Sammy had always protected Mark and loved him, but she would steal his peanut butter sandwiches any chance she got. Ticker always licked Mark's face until he giggled and pushed him away.

As the spring changed slowly to summer, we resigned ourselves to the fact that our friends were gone. We would never quit looking for them and we would never forget them. Slowly and sadly we turned back once again to our ranch work.

EPILOGUE

A YEAR AFTER TICKER and Sammy disappeared, I decided to leave big outfit cowboying and move my family to the eastern slopes of the Rockies. Mark needed a school and I needed to spend more time at home with him and Chris.

I took work in southern Alberta and was able to stay in the cattle business as well as have my family close to a town. It had been a long time for us to be away, and we were glad to be back in civilization.

We left a different and unique lifestyle behind us. Ours had been a big oufit world with cowboys and horses, cattle and fences, endless miles of country to prowl with deer, bears and wolves. Large cattle ranches did whatever they had to do in today's world to remain afloat.

In so many ways it was hard, yet in many more ways it was easy. As you learned to challenge yourself and gain rewards from meeting those challenges, you became stronger.

Sometimes now, when I'm by myself, I look west towards those forbidding, silent mountains. Locked away behind their stone walls is a big part of my life. It is almost as if that part of me didn't really exist. It was someone else—not me—and Patch, Bossdog, Ticker and Sammy weren't real either. Did we really live and punch cows and play together? They were such good friends and now they're gone. A lonely feeling drifts over me like the wind blowing sadly through an old abandoned cabin in some forgotten meadow. I wish I could go back and be with them for just one more day.

Ranch people are often admired for their strength, courage and positive outlook. They spend countless days with animals that depend on them for everything, constantly witnessing the everlasting cycle of life. They see things born and watch them die. They do what can be done to stop animals from dying and sometimes find out that it's not enough. They learn to accept death because they have seen it and tried to stop it but it happens anyway.

So they learn to love things while they are still alive.

GLOSSARY OF TERMS

CAVVY The main bunch of broke saddle horses that accompany the cowboys to the various camps.

CHINKS Short leather chaps or leggings.

CINCH UP Tighten up the saddle.

COWBOSS The lead hand or foreman of the crew.

CULLS Cattle that have been sorted off the main herd and are designated for slaughter.

DALLY To take a wrap around the saddlehorn with a rope.

DEAD PIT A large hole excavated in a secluded area and used to dispose of garbage and dead animals.

DRAW A gully or ravine.

DUMMY	An apparatus built to simulate a calf with a head and legs. Used for roping practice on the ground.
FALL WORKS	All the gathering, sorting and shipping work that takes place during the busy fall season.
FEEDLOT	An operation that feeds cattle in close confines until they reach slaughter weight.
FETLOCK	Ankle area of horse.
FRIJOLES	A Mexican dish of beans and whatever else is handy to throw in.
GATHER	To bunch or assemble a head of cattle.
GRADE COW	Cross bred or commercial cow. Not a purebred, but one of mixed lineage.
GREEN	New, inexperienced.
HEIFER	Young female cow under two years of age.
HONDA	Cowboy's rope that allows the main part of the rope to feed through it.
JIGGERBOSS	Second in command after the cowboss.
JINGLE	Daily task of bringing in the cavvy or saddlehorse bunch.
LEPPIE CALF	Orphaned calf that has survived on its own in the herd.

LINED OUT	Trot away from.
NINE-O	Very fast. Rodeo term referring to 9.0 seconds which is fast.
NUMBER NINE	A cow will throw its tail up high and it will bend over up at the top, creating a number '9'. This happens a split second before the animal breaks and runs.
RE-RIDES	To straggle or go back through an area for a second or third time to check for cattle that may have been missed.
RIGGING	Term referring to saddles or horse gear.
RIM OUT	To leave, quit the country, head out.
RODEAR	A gathering or bunching of cattle in a designated spot.
ROO-BAR	A metal bumper that surrounds the front of an Australian truck to protect it from kangaroos that may be hit on the backroads of Australia.
SCOURS	Dysentery in calves.
SHITTER	Horse.
SILAGE	Chopped and cured forage.
SLASH PILE	Huge piles of branches and debris from logged-off areas.
STEERS	Castrated male cattle.

STRAGGLE	Re-ride.
STRIP CALVES	Separate the calves from the cows.
SUCKERED	Led to believe, conned into.
TEAM-ROPING	A rodeo event involving a "header" who ropes the animal by the head and a "heeler" who ropes the heels. The animal is then stretched out between the two cowboys.
TO BE WORKED	Sorted, the cattle need to be worked.
TWINE	Refers to a cowboy's rope. Slang term.
TURNOUT	Cattle are "turned out" in the summer to graze on selected open grazing leases or permits in ranch country.
WAGON BOSS	Cowboy foreman of a mobile cowboy wagon unit.
WARBAG	Personal possessions duffelbag.
WEAN	To separate calves from the cows.
WILDRAGS	Scarves or neckerchiefs worn by cowboys.
WILLIAMS LAKE STAMPEDE	Major rodeo and celebration in the town of Williams Lake, BC. Infamous as a wild time.

INDEX